THE STARGAZER'S GUIDE TO THE GALAXY

By Q. L. Pearce

Illustrated by Mary Ann Fraser

TOR

A TOM DOHERTY ASSOCIATES BOOK
NEW YORK

To my all-stars: Lahaina,
Shiloh, and Chatelet
　　　　　　　　　—Q.L.P.

To Douglas Fraser, for your
part in Desert Storm
　　　　　　　　　—M.A.F.

A Tor Book
Published by Tom Doherty Associates, Inc.
49 West 24th Street
New York, NY 10010

Illustrated by Mary Ann Fraser

ISBN: 0-812-59423-1

First trade paper edition: September 1991

Printed in the United States of America

0   9   8   7   6   5   4   3   2   1

Table of Contents

An Introduction to Nighttime Viewing

Guideposts in the Sky

Have you ever looked up at the night sky and wondered how many stars there are? There seem to be thousands. In fact, the universe contains trillions and trillions of stars. Most are too faint or far away for us to see, even with a telescope. On a clear, dark night, you can usually see up to two thousand stars with your naked eye.

Humans have always been curious about the heavens. Cave paintings of 30,000 years ago plotted the path of the Moon through the seasons of the year. Nearly 5,000 years ago, the Sumerians and Egyptians decided what crops to plant and when to plant them based on which stars were rising or setting at the time. Using plenty of imagination, ancient peoples of many cultures "connected" groups of stars to form patterns, like huge dot-to-dot puzzles. They named these groups, or **constellations** (kon-steh-LAY-shunz), after characters from their stories and myths.

Since 1922, astronomers around the world have agreed to and mapped 88 constellations. Because each constellation has a distinct boundary in the sky, they serve as "guideposts" for locating celestial objects within them. In the same way that you would look at a map of the state of California to locate the city of Los Angeles, you would look at a star map of the constellation **Orion** (or-EYE-on) to locate the supergiant star *Rigel* (RY-jel).

Viewing with the Unaided Eye, Telescopes, and Binoculars

Not all of the 88 constellations are visible from any one place on Earth. Your view of the night sky depends on your location on the planet. If you live in New York, for example, you cannot see many of the constellations that twinkle above Melbourne, Australia. Most constellations are visible to the naked (or unaided) eye—but to see certain constellations, which are made up of fainter stars, you may want to use binoculars or a telescope. The great astronomer Galileo (gal-uh-LAY-o) made many amazing discoveries using a simple telescope.

There are two main types of telescope: the **refracting telescope** and the **reflecting telescope**. Both types collect light and magnify images. By doing so, they make dim objects appear to be brighter, and distant objects (like stars) appear to be larger and closer to the viewer.

REFRACTING TELESCOPE

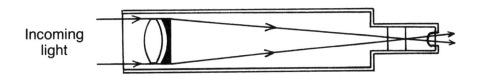

Incoming
light

The refracting telescope is thought to have been developed in 1608 by a Dutch spectacle-maker named Hans Lippershey. Galileo first used a refracting telescope two years later, in 1610. Light from the object being viewed enters at one end through the **objective lens**, which is thick in the center and thin around the edge. This lens bends the light inward to form an image. At the other end, a smaller lens called the **eyepiece** enlarges the image.

Hipparchus was an astronomer born in Asia Minor. The dates of his birth and death are unknown but he lived roughly between 146 B.C. and 127 B.C. Even though there were no telescopes or binoculars then, Hipparchus catalogued the positions of more than 850 stars. He also "graded" their brightness from one to six: the brightest stars were number one, and the faintest stars were number six.

NEWTONIAN REFLECTING TELESCOPE

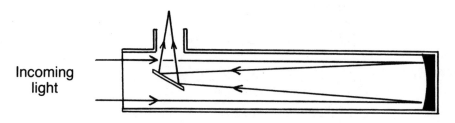

Incoming
light

The reflecting telescope was invented by Isaac Newton and was introduced in 1671. Light enters at one end and travels to the opposite end, where it is collected by a curved **primary mirror**. The light is then reflected back toward the front of the telescope, where it gathers to produce an image. A **secondary mirror** then reflects the image to the side, where it is magnified by the eyepiece in the side of the telescope tube.

Binoculars are really two small refracting telescopes, but with several glass wedges called **prisms** in the tubes. These prisms ensure that the image will be right side up. Binoculars are easy to carry and use, and through them you can see a large area of the sky at one time.

When stargazing with the naked eye, binoculars, or a telescope, your view may be diminished by smog, cloud cover, and city lights. Also, the constant motion of Earth's air can prevent you from getting a clear picture of the stars. As starlight passes through warm and cold layers of unsteady air, it bends and appears to flicker or twinkle. Because the planets are so much closer to us than the stars are, they appear larger so the light reflected from them is generally steadier. However, on a very windy night, planets, too, can appear to twinkle.

The Moon

Only 240,000 miles from Earth, the **Moon** is an ideal place to start your tour of the universe. Dark plains on the lunar surface are clear to the naked eye. Called "seas" (or, in Latin, *mare*), these were formed millions of years ago as molten rock gushed through cracks in the Moon's crust and hardened. The first humans to visit the Moon landed in the Sea of Tranquility on July 20, 1969, during the Apollo 11 mission.

Because the time the Moon takes to rotate once on its axis—$27\frac{1}{3}$ days—is the same time it takes to complete one orbit around the Earth, we always see the same side of the Moon. However, our nearest neighbor doesn't always look the same. Just like the Earth, half of the lunar surface is always lit by the Sun, but as the Moon

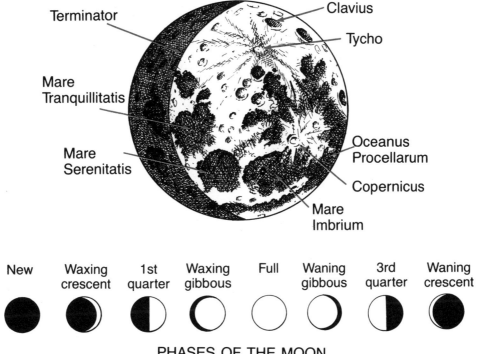

| New | Waxing crescent | 1st quarter | Waxing gibbous | Full | Waning gibbous | 3rd quarter | Waning crescent |

PHASES OF THE MOON

travels around the Earth, we see different amounts of the sunlit area. The changing amounts we see of that sunlit area are called **phases**. The dividing line between dark and light during such a phase is called the **terminator**. All along the terminator, surface features such as mountain ranges and craters cast dark shadows onto the sunlit side and are easy to spot with a telescope. During a full Moon, it is difficult to observe details on the bright, shadowless lunar face.

There are more than 300,000 meteorite craters on the near side of the Moon. The crater Copernicus, nearly 60 miles across and with walls 2 miles high, is one of the most impressive. Its outer ridge rises 2,700 feet from base to tip. The collision that formed Copernicus also scattered dusty material that appears to flare outward from the crater as bright rays. Unlike other features, these rays are clearly visible during a full Moon.

Nicolaus Copernicus (1473–1543) was a Polish astronomer. For hundreds of years before Copernicus's time, astronomers had believed that the Earth stood still in space and that the Sun, stars, and planets revolved around it. Copernicus believed, and eventually demonstrated, that the Earth rotated on its **axis** (an imaginary line drawn through the planet from the North Pole to the South Pole), and that all of the planets revolved around the Sun.

The Planets

The **solar system** is our "neighborhood" in space. It is made up of the Sun and everything that revolves around it, including all of the planets and their moons, as well as comets, asteroids, and other bodies. Of the nine known planets in our solar family, six can sometimes be seen from Earth with the unaided eye. You will need to either call a planetarium or look up monthly sky chart information in an astronomy magazine (such as *Odyssey* or *Sky and Telescope*) to know where in the sky to look for each of the visible planets and at which time of year. Over just a few days or weeks, all the planets change their positions in the sky in relation to the stars. In fact, the word *planet* comes from a Greek word that means "wanderer."

 Mercury orbits very close to the Sun, making it difficult to see from Earth. You can sometimes catch a glimpse of it low in the west at sunset or in the east just before sunrise. With a telescope and patience, you may observe that, like our Moon, Mercury goes through phases.

 A lifeless, desert world with little or no atmosphere to hold in heat, Mercury experiences the widest range of temperatures in the solar system. Temperatures reach about 800° Fahrenheit during the day and plummet at night to −300°F. Mercury also has the fastest orbital speed of all the planets, racing around the Sun at about 107,000 miles per hour. Its year is only 88 Earth days long.

 With the exception of the Moon, **Venus** is the most brilliant object in Earth's night sky. Like the Moon and Mercury, this planet goes through phases as it journeys around the Sun. Venus is similar in size to the Earth, but it is much hotter because of its dense atmosphere, which is 90 times thicker than ours. Temperatures on Venus can reach 900°F, which is hot enough to melt lead. The rocky surface of the planet is completely hidden from view by layers of pale clouds.

 Mars appears as a brilliant, reddish-white dot in the night sky. Much of the planet is covered by reddish rocks and dust. About 100 years ago, astronomers studying the planet reported seeing long, straight lines cutting across the surface. Some scientists interpreted these as canals, perhaps built by intelligent Martians. Information from interplanetary probes such as the Viking spacecraft now has proved that the canals were optical illusions, the product of overactive imaginations. Depending on how close Mars is to Earth, however, through a telescope you can observe dark and light areas on the planet, as well as the glittering polar ice caps.

 Jupiter, the largest of the planets, is easy to spot with the naked eye. Using binoculars, you can see colorful "bands" caused by tremendous wind currents ripping through the planet's atmosphere. Swirling storms are also visible. One continuous storm, known as the **Great Red Spot**, is large enough to swallow the entire Earth. This storm has been raging for at least 350 years, since Galileo first studied Jupiter through his telescope.

JUPITER

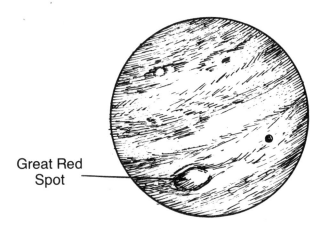

Great Red
Spot

It is easy to distinguish huge **Saturn** by the strikingly beautiful system of rings circling it. Until Voyager's famous journey, scientists thought that Saturn's rings were unique. Now we know that all of the giant gas planets—Jupiter, Saturn, Uranus, and Neptune—have at least slender rings.

Of the outermost planets, **Uranus**, **Neptune**, and rocky **Pluto**, only Uranus can be seen with the naked eye, and even under ideal conditions, it still appears as a very faint dot of light.

SATURN

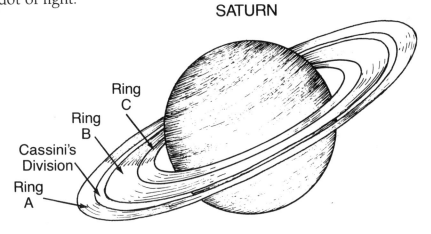

Ring
C

Ring
B

Cassini's
Division

Ring
A

Tycho Brahe (1546–1601), a Danish astronomer, made very precise observations of the stars and planets from an observatory on the tiny Danish island of Hven. He did not agree with Copernicus's theory that the planets revolved around the Sun. In fact, he hired an assistant named Johannes Kepler to help him disprove it. Instead, Kepler's work helped to prove that Copernicus was right.

Moons and Rings

Our Moon is one of dozens of moons in our solar system. Mercury and Venus do not have moons, but all of the other planets do. Several of these moons are easy to view from Earth. Jupiter has at least 16 moons, 4 of which are known as the Galilean (gal-uh-LAY-un) moons because they were discovered by Galileo. On brilliant, orange-red **Io** (EYE-o), huge volcanoes spew gas and dust more than 100 miles into space. The icy surface of the bright Galilean moon, **Europa** (yoo-ROH-puh), is riddled with cracks and streaks, but because it has no mountains or valleys, Europa is the smoothest object in the solar system. Nearly 3,300 miles wide, **Ganymede** (GAN-uh-meed), the solar system's largest moon, is bigger than the planets Mercury and Pluto. The darkest of the Galilean moons, **Callisto** (kuh-LIS-toh), is also the most heavily cratered object in our solar family.

 Titan (TYT-un), at about 3,200 miles in diameter, is the largest of Saturn's 17 known moons. The temperature on Titan is a frigid −288°F. Although it is much colder, this moon, cloaked in a dense, orange-tinted atmosphere, is similar to our primitive Earth of several billion years ago.

 All of the gas planets are circled by some sort of ring system. The ring system of Saturn, however, is the most spectacular. Made up of rocks, dust, and ice, Saturn's rings actually consist of *thousands* of ringlets. Although the rings are 175,000 miles wide—two-thirds the distance from the Earth to the Moon—they are very flat at just two miles thick. You will need a telescope to observe these remarkable rings.

Asteroids

Asteroids (AS-ter-oydz) are small rocky objects, typically a mile or two across, that did not form into planets during the creation of the solar system. Most circle the Sun in orbits between Mars and Jupiter. Two large clusters of asteroids actually share Jupiter's orbit; these clusters are generally known as the **Trojan** asteroids and are named after heroes of the Trojan Wars.

 Ceres (SEER-eez), which at 580 miles in diameter is the largest known asteroid, was discovered in 1801. Similar bodies were sighted soon after, and British astronomer William Herschel (HER-shul) suggested they be called asteroids, which means "starlike." At least 4,500 have been identified. Most asteroids are small—altogether they wouldn't make up a planet as large as our Moon! The brightest asteroid, **Vesta** (VES-tuh), is the only one that can sometimes be seen from Earth with the naked eye, but at least 100 can be seen with a small telescope.

Perhaps the most interesting asteroids are the **Apollos**. Called "Earth approachers," these bodies often approach or even cross our own planet's orbit. More than 100 of these asteroids are known. The closest pass yet recorded took place on January 18, 1991. An asteroid some 25 feet across and traveling at 36,000 miles per hour zoomed past the Earth at a distance of only 100,000 miles—less than half the distance to the Moon.

Comets

Beyond the planets billions, perhaps even trillions, of **comets** are believed to lie in an immense cluster known as the **Oort cloud**. Occasionally, something such as the gravity of a passing star "nudges" a comet out of the Oort cloud and causes it to pass within the orbits of the planets. Comets are dark, cold balls of ice and dust. They are probably made of material leftover from the formation of the solar system. As a comet moves closer to the heat and light of the Sun, it develops a halo, or **coma** (KO-muh), of gas. At this time it may appear to a viewer on Earth as a small, hazy object moving through the night sky. As it draws closer to the Sun, the comet may develop a long, flowing tail of gas streaming out behind it. It will also often have a curved dust tail. The gas tails are sometimes visible to an Earth observer. The longest tail ever recorded, sighted in 1843, extended nearly 200 million miles! Not all comets are so spectacular, and few can be seen without a telescope.

Halley's comet, named for the astronomer who first predicted its orbit, is probably the best-known comet. It dashes past Earth every 76 years on its long journey around the Sun; its next flyby will occur in the year 2061. With each orbit, this comet loses about three feet of its surface as it is boiled away by the Sun's heat. Even though Halley's dark, potato-shaped center, or **nucleus**, is about the size of Manhattan, it will probably survive only about one thousand more trips before it disintegrates.

Galileo Galilei (1564–1642) was the first astronomer to use a telescope. On January 7, 1610, this great Italian scientist discovered three of the largest moons of Jupiter. On January 13, he discovered a fourth. He also discovered that there were mountains, valleys, and craters on Earth's moon, and that the Milky Way galaxy was made up of millions of stars.

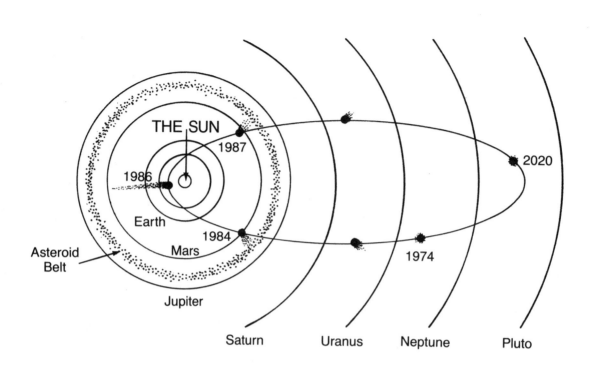

Meteoroids

Meteoroids are chunks of rock and dust, perhaps dust from a comet's tail or remnants of a collision between asteroids. Meteoroids do not necessarily have fixed orbits, but usually follow random paths through space. Each day about 400 tons of this dust and gravel tumble into Earth's atmosphere. As particles plunge earthward at speeds of up to 20 miles per second, they heat up and leave behind a glowing streak of light. The light trail, often called a "shooting star," is a **meteor**. Even tiny grains of dust can put on a remarkable show in the night sky—a **meteor shower**. In its orbit around the Sun, the Earth regularly passes through dust tails left behind by comets. At these times, many more meteoroids than usual enter our atmosphere. Meteor showers appear to originate from one central spot, or **radiant point**, and so are named for the constellation in which the point is found.

Meteoroids that survive the fiery fall and actually land on Earth are called **meteorites**. Most are quite small, but a few are astoundingly large. A meteorite that crashed about 50,000 years ago in what is now Arizona created the Barringer (or Meteor) Crater, which is 4,150 feet wide and 570 feet deep. Scientists calculate that the meteorite must have weighed about 300,000 tons!

METEOR SHOWER

The Sun

The Sun, the center of our solar system, is a **star**. Stars are churning, fiery balls of gas, mostly hydrogen, and ours is no different. The Sun's diameter is more than 100 times that of our planet, and it is large enough to contain more than one million Earths! Almost half of the Sun's mass is in its center, or **core**, where temperatures reach 25 million degrees Fahrenheit. The tremendous heat and pressure there cause hydrogen to change into another element, helium, in a reaction known as **fusion** (FYOO-zhun). This reaction produces energy that radiates in all directions. Without heat and light from the Sun, life on Earth could not exist.

   The Sun's atmosphere is made up of three layers. The innermost layer of the atmosphere is the bubbling **photosphere**. At times, huge, dark, "cooler" areas called **sunspots** form in this photosphere. From the middle layer, the **chromosphere**,

---

Johannes Kepler (1571–1630), a German astronomer, is famous for his three laws of planetary motion. These laws describe how the planets move in their orbits. Kepler showed that the planets travel around the Sun in elliptical (sort of oval-shaped) orbits.

THE SUN'S ATMOSPHERE

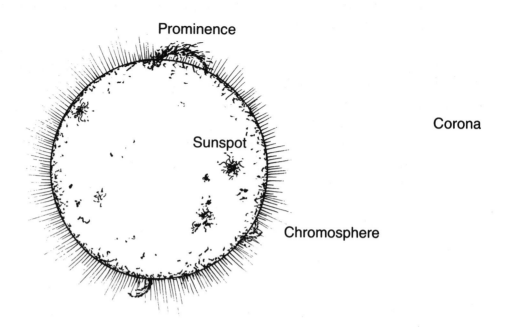

blazing fountains of gas called **prominences** arc thousands of miles into space. From the outermost layer, the **corona**, particles of hydrogen atoms flow into space and make up the **solar wind**.

WARNING! NEVER LOOK DIRECTLY AT THE SUN THROUGH A TELESCOPE OR BINOCULARS! It is very dangerous to look directly at the Sun, and viewing it through an unfiltered telescope can result in permanent blindness. Even when a telescope is filtered, it is not necessarily safe. Don't take chances! If you want to see the sunspots or observe an eclipse, call a local planetarium. It might offer special sessions to view the Sun.

The Stars

Stars, like people, come in different sizes and colors. A star's color depends on its temperature, which in turn usually depends on how massive the star is. **Mass** and size are not the same. Mass is the amount of material that makes up an object. Two things can be the same size but of unequal mass. For example, a bowling ball, a volleyball, and a balloon may be similar in size, but the bowling ball has the most mass.

Brightness, or **magnitude** (MAG-nih-tood), is one way that we can identify or locate certain stars. How bright a star looks to us depends not only on its **absolute magnitude** (that is, its actual brightness), but also on its distance from Earth. For example, *Sirius* (SEER-ee-us) is not the brightest star in the galaxy, but since it is closer to us than most other stars, it *appears* to be the brightest in the sky. This is called **apparent magnitude**.

In the second century B.C., the Greek astronomer Hipparchus divided the stars into six categories of apparent magnitude, with 1.0 being the brightest. Since the time of Hipparchus, some stars have been discovered to be even brighter than the upper limit of the scale. These stars have been given the number 0 or a negative number (such as −0.6). Modern astronomers still rely on this useful scale.

To residents of Earth, the Sun is the most important star in the sky. But compared with the other stars, it is not very special. About 99 percent of the stars you see with the naked eye are larger and brighter than our Sun.

The Brightest Stars in the Night Sky

Name	Magnitude	Distance (in light-years)	Color	Constellation
Sirius	−1.5	8.7	blue-white	**Canis Major**
Arcturus	−0.06	36	orange	**Boötes**
Vega	0.0	27	blue-white	**Lyra**
Capella	0.1	45	yellow-white	**Auriga**
Rigel	0.1	900	blue-white	**Orion**
Aldebaran	0.8	68	red-orange	**Taurus**
Spica	1.0	220	blue	**Virgo**

Christian Huygens (1629–1695) was a Dutch astronomer who worked with lenses and made his own very powerful telescope. He showed that the funny "handles" that Galileo had observed around Saturn were actually rings.

The Lives of Stars

A **nebula** (NEB-yoo-luh) is a cloud of dust and gas (mostly hydrogen) in space. These large bodies are sometimes called "stellar nurseries" (the word *stellar* is used to describe stars). Scientists believe that, occasionally, something (the effect of a supernova, for example) causes the gas and dust to draw together in huge clumps within a cloud. Gravity causes the clumps to collapse in on themselves, to attract more material, and to grow hotter and hotter until, thousands of years later, the core reaches a temperature of about 15 million degrees Celsius. Fusion then begins, the core material ignites, and a star is born.

A star such as our yellow Sun generally burns for about 10 billion years before it uses up most of its fuel supply. Toward the end of its life, the Sun will swell into a **red giant**, then collapse into a **white dwarf** (about the size of the Earth), and finally burn out. Stars more massive than the Sun have a shorter life and may come to a different end. In its final stages, such a massive star might expand into a **red supergiant**. Some explode, in a tremendous blast known as a **supernova**, which hurls dust and gas millions of miles in every direction. The remains of the original star may become a **neutron star**. These small stars are as small as ten miles in diameter but are incredibly dense. If the original star was extremely large, the neutron star may continue to collapse, creating what is known as a **black hole**. Black holes are so massive and have such intense gravity that nothing, not even light, can escape, and so they cannot be seen.

	Constellation Key
⬯	Galaxy
○⦿	Variable star > magnitude 5
⁜	Open cluster
⬚	Globular cluster
⧄	Dark nebula
▢	Planetary nebula

Unimaginable Distances

A galaxy is a huge group of stars bound together by their gravitational pull on one another. Our solar system is part of the **Milky Way galaxy**. The distances between stars and galaxies are so great that scientists use light rather than miles to describe them. Light travels faster than anything else known. A **light-year**, the distance that light travels in one year, is about 6 trillion miles. The Sun is 93 million miles from Earth. That is a distance of only 8 **light-minutes**. You would have to make 32,000 round trips to the Sun and back to travel the distance of one light-year! After our Sun, the nearest star to Earth is *Proxima Centauri* (PROK-suh-muh sen-TAWR-ee), which is more than 4 light-years away. The nearest galaxy visible from the northern hemisphere, Andromeda (an-DROM-ud-uh), is more than *2 million* light-years away!

The Milky Way galaxy is about 100,000 light-years across. Our solar system is located about two-thirds of the way out from the center, in a long spiral arm of this galaxy. If you look toward the constellation **Sagittarius**, you are looking toward the center of the galaxy. On a dark, moonless night you can see the galactic center as a path of light (also known as the Milky Way) that appears to arc high across the sky.

From Our Point of View

If you watch the night sky for several hours, you will see the stars appear to drift slowly from east to west. This effect is caused by the movement of the Earth as it spins, or rotates, on its axis. The Sun also seems to travel across the sky on an imaginary path called the **ecliptic** (ih-KLIP-tik). The constellations that form the background for this path are called the constellations of the **zodiac** (ZO-dee-ak). The word *zodiac* is from a Greek phrase that means "circle of animals," and all but one of the 12 traditional constellations of the zodiac are represented by animals. The Moon and planets, too, can always be found close to the ecliptic and within the zodiac.

When we say the Sun is "in" a certain constellation, we mean that, if you could see the stars during the day, that constellation would appear to be the "backdrop" for the Sun and would seem to accompany the Sun across the sky in its daily journey. The

Isaac Newton (1642–1727), of England, was one of the greatest scientists who ever lived. He discovered the law of gravity and developed calculus, a form of mathematics that is of great importance to astronomers and other scientists. Newton also described the nature of light and invented the reflecting telescope.

Sun, however, lags a little. It takes the Sun four minutes longer to complete its daily journey than it takes the stars. That lag time adds up, and after about four to six weeks, the next zodiac constellation catches up to the Sun, and the Sun "enters" the borders of that constellation. It is then "in" that constellation for several weeks.

Because our planet revolves, or orbits, around the Sun, our view of the night sky is always changing. To make it easier for you to figure out which constellations you will see at different times of the year, this book provides a new star map for each season. Keep in mind that the star groups pictured in these maps are not all drawn to the same scale. For example, **Corona Borealis**, mentioned on page 40, is a very small constellation, while **Ursa Major** (page 24) stretches far across the sky.

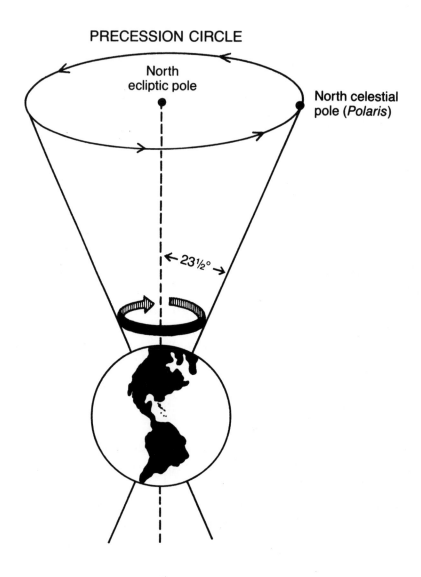

PRECESSION CIRCLE

North ecliptic pole

North celestial pole (*Polaris*)

23½°

The North Star

Although the night sky seems to be always moving and changing, one star appears to stay fixed in the same place. This star is *Polaris* (po-LAIR-iss), or the North Star or **polestar**. How high above the horizon *Polaris* is depends on where you live. The farther north you are, the higher in the sky it will appear. If you were standing at the North Pole, this star would be overhead. *Polaris* seems to stay in one place because Earth's **axis** (an imaginary line running through the planet from pole to pole) points almost directly at it. For hundreds of years, sailors in the northern hemisphere have been able to set a course at night by using the reliable position of this star.

Eventually, the movement of our planet will cause *Polaris* to appear to wander. Our spinning planet wobbles slightly like a top. The wobble is very slow and takes 26,000 years to complete one turn. During that wobble the Earth's axis slowly sweeps a circle in the sky, pointing at different stars along its path. Five thousand years ago, a star named *Thuban* (THOO-ban) was the polestar. During the time of the Trojan War, two other stars, *Pherkad* (FUR-kad) and *Kochab* (KO-kab), were nearest to the place of honor and were called the Guardians of the Pole. This movement of the axis among the stars is called **precession**. For several hundreds of years to come, Polaris will be a reliable beacon in the night sky, but someday another star will be the North Star.

The Big Dipper

A reliable guide to the night sky at any time of year is the **Big Dipper**, a star group that looks something like a huge, long-handled water ladle. Throughout the year, the Big Dipper appears to rotate around the North Star with its bowl always facing inward. (In the southernmost states of the United States, this star group takes a brief early evening "dip" below the horizon in autumn.) Before starting your visual journey of the sky, study the appropriate seasonal star map in this book and become familiar with the Big Dipper's position in the sky.

Edmund Halley (1656–1742) was the first person to figure out that the comets in our solar system actually orbited around the Sun. Using the theory of gravity just published by Newton, Halley plotted the orbit of a particular comet and predicted when it would reappear. Although he died before the comet returned, Halley was correct, and the comet was named after him.

THE BIG DIPPER'S ROTATION AROUND *POLARIS*
(mid-northern latitudes)

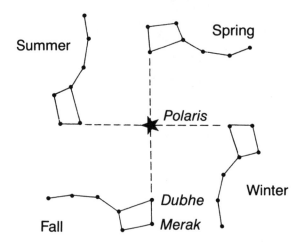

When you are ready to begin, go outside and face west. (That is where the Sun sets at the end of the day.) Turn your head and look in the direction of your right shoulder. This is approximately north. (Unless you are at the North Pole, the Big Dipper will appear in the northern sky.) Now locate the Big Dipper, which is about 25 degrees long and easy to spot. (A degree is a measure of distance.) Two bright stars at the front of the scoop, *Merak* (MEE-rak) and *Dubhe* (DOO-bee), are called the **pointers**. If you draw a line through them it will point toward *Polaris*. During different seasons, the Big Dipper can help you find many other important stars. By using it as a guide, you can "star-hop" from one constellation to another.

Taking a Look

The constellations in this book are bright or fairly bright groups of stars that can be seen from mid-northern latitudes. That includes most areas of the United States. **Latitude** is used to describe position north or south of Earth's equator. It is measured in **degrees** with the equator at 0 degrees and the North Pole at 90 degrees north latitude.

William Herschel (1738–1822) was a German-born astronomer who lived in England. He discovered the planet Uranus. He also proposed that our solar system is a part of the Milky Way galaxy.

The sky, too, can be measured in degrees. You have a handy measuring device right at the end of your outstretched arm—your hand. The distance from the horizon to the point directly overhead (the **zenith**) is 90 degrees. When you hold your arm out, the end of your little finger covers about one degree of night sky. The width of your first three fingers is about 5 degrees, your closed fist equals about 10 degrees, and the spread between your index and little finger is 15 degrees.

In this book you will find star maps for each season. Each shows an east and west view of the night sky. If you are not sure how to find east and west, just watch the Sun, which rises in the east and sets in the west.

You will be able to see many more stars on a clear, moonless night away from the glare of city lights. If you can, find a place without many trees or buildings in the way. It takes about 15 minutes for your eyes to adjust to the darkness. If you use a flashlight, cover it with red cellophane so the glare will not affect your darkness-adjusted vision.

Charles Messier (1730–1817) was a French astronomer who was extremely interested in comets. As he searched the night skies he noted many blurs of light that looked like, but were not, comets. To prevent confusion, he compiled a catalog of more than 100 of these objects and assigned each a number. Since that time, scientists have determined that these objects are star clusters, galaxies, and nebulae, and they still identify most by their Messier, or "M," number.

Spring Star Map
(March–June)

How to use this map:

Turn this star map so that the direction you face matches the direction of the constellations you can read. An easy way to do this is to identify known stars close to the horizon and then line up your map.

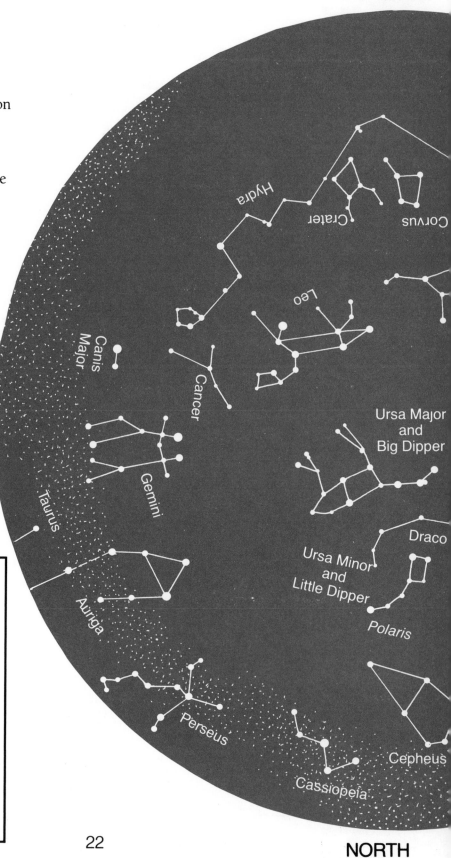

WEST

Hydra

Crater

Corvus

Canis Major

Cancer

Leo

Ursa Major and Big Dipper

Gemini

Taurus

Draco

Ursa Minor and Little Dipper

Auriga

Polaris

Perseus

Cepheus

Cassiopeia

NORTH

Scale of Star Magnitudes: Seasonal Star Charts

- ● 0–1   First and most bright
- ● 2   Second brightest
- ● 3   Third brightest
- • 4   Fourth brightest
- · 5   Fifth and least bright

       Milky Way

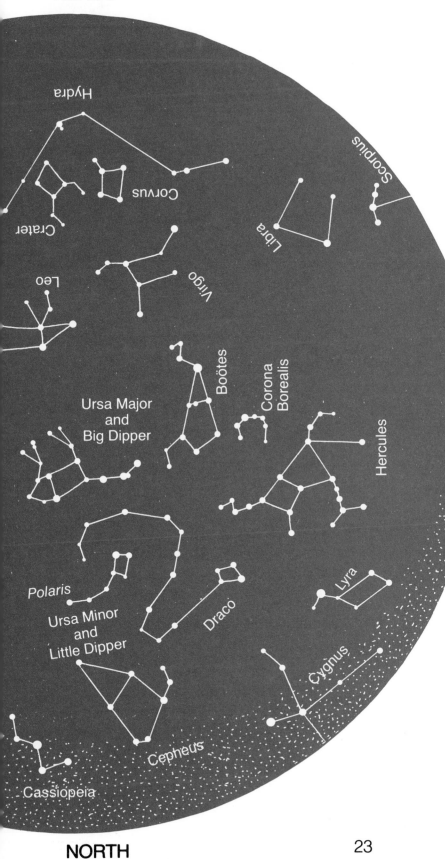

Hydra

Corvus

Crater

Leo

Virgo

Libra

Scorpius

Boötes

Corona Borealis

Ursa Major and Big Dipper

Hercules

Polaris

Ursa Minor and Little Dipper

Draco

Lyra

Cygnus

Cepheus

Cassiopeia

EAST

Late March	12 p.m.
Early April	11 p.m.
Late April	10 p.m.
Early May	9 p.m.
Late May	8 p.m.
Early June	7 p.m.

Add one hour for daylight-saving time

Scale of Star Magnitudes: Individual Star Maps

- ● 0–1 First and most bright
- ● 2 Second brightest
- ● 3 Third brightest
- ● 4 Fourth brightest
- • 5 Fifth brightest
- · 6+ Sixth and least bright

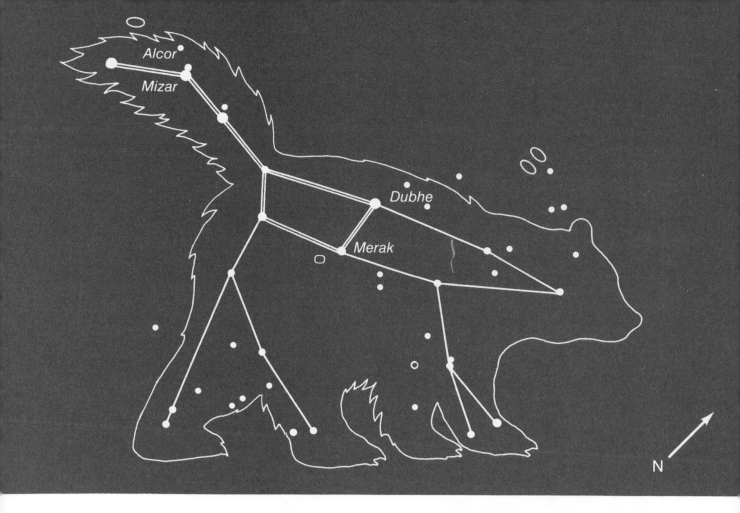

Ursa Major
The Great Bear

The Big Dipper

The Big Dipper is one of the easiest groups of stars to find, but it isn't an official constellation. It is a part of the constellation **Ursa Major**, the Great Bear. The handle of the dipper marks the long tail of this huge bear. Two stars in the middle of the handle, *Mizar* (MEE-zar) and *Alcor* (AL-kor), form an **optical double star**—that is, two stars that only *appear* to be very close together. These stars are not actually physically near each other. They just appear to be so because they are both in the same line of sight of an observer on Earth.

To the North American Housatonic Indians, **Ursa Major** represents a great star bear that was once wounded in a hunt. According to the legend, blood drips from the wound every fall, staining Earth's forests with red. The Blackfoot Indians tell a different tale about the seven stars that make up the Big Dipper. Taking the form of a bear, an evil woman chased her seven brothers and younger sister. Before she could harm them, one brother shot eight magical arrows into the sky and each boy became a distant star in the Big Dipper, while the sister became the faint star *Alcor*.

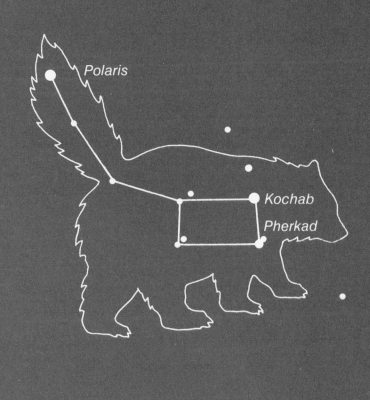

Polaris

Kochab

Pherkad

Ursa Minor
The Little Bear

The Little Dipper

According to a Greek myth, the *Great* Bear was once a woman named Callisto (kuh-LIST-o). The powerful Greek god Zeus (ZOOS) fell in love with her, so his jealous wife, Hera (HAIR-uh), turned Callisto into a bear. Years later, Callisto's son, Arcas (AR-kus), met what he thought was a bear in the woods. Not knowing it was his mother, he aimed his bow and arrow at her. To save Callisto, Zeus turned Arcas into a bear, too—the *Little* Bear. Then he grabbed them both by their tails and pulled them into the heavens, where we see them today as **Ursa Major** and **Ursa Minor**. Because Zeus tugged so hard, the bears' tails stretched, and that is why both bears have such long tails.

The Little Dipper is a part of **Ursa Minor**. Its handle is the bear's tail, with *Polaris*, the North Star, glittering at the tip. A white supergiant with a magnitude of 2.0, *Polaris* is about 50 times larger than our Sun! About 600 light-years distant, *Polaris* is a **cepheid variable star**, which means that it dims and brightens slightly at intervals. Its pattern repeats about every four days.

25

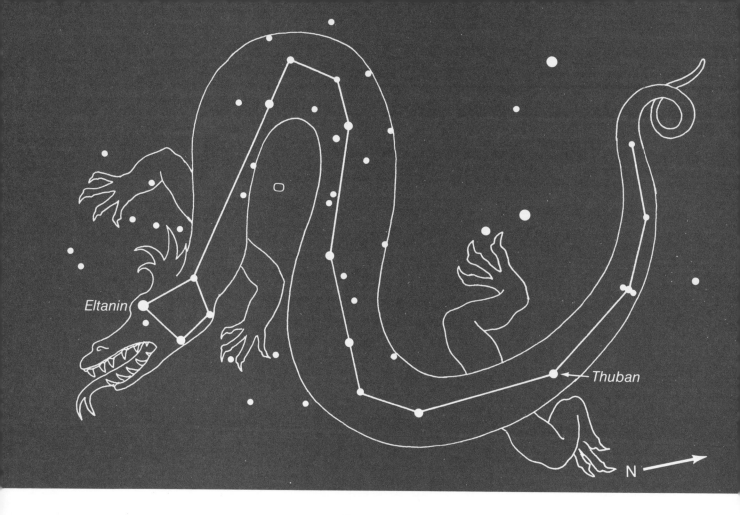

Draco
The Dragon

According to a nearly three-thousand-year-old legend from ancient Babylon, when the Earth was young there were two groups of gods. The older gods wanted to rest and the younger ones wanted to play. The leader of the young gods, Marduk (MAR-dook), finally met Tiamat (TYAH-maht), the leader of the old gods, in battle. Although Tiamat appeared in the form of a horrible dragon, Marduk defeated her. He left her body in the heavens as a reminder of the terrible combat.

This starry beast can be found between the Big Dipper and the Little Dipper. In its tail is *Thuban* (THOO-ban). (*Thuban* was the polestar 5,000 years ago and will take up this celestial position again 20,000 years from now.) In the dragon's head is another bright star, the yellow giant *Eltanin* (el-TAY-nin). Around January 3, the radiant point for the Quantrantid (kwan-TRAN-tid) meteor shower can be found above Draco's head.

26

Arcturus

N

Boötes
The Herdsman

The Greeks believed that **Boötes** (boo-OH-teez) was a herdsman named Icarius (ih-KAIR-ee-us). He was a dear friend of the god of wine, Dionysus (dy-o-NY-sus). Icarius was killed by enemies, and his body was hidden under a tree. Dionysus found his lost friend and honored him by placing him in the stars. The Egyptians also believed that **Boötes** was a herdsman, but that he was put in the heavens to guard Earth against the Great Bear lurking nearby.

To find this constellation, follow the handle of the Big Dipper. It arcs toward *Arcturus* (ark-TOOR-us), the brightest star in **Boötes** and the fourth brightest in the night sky. *Arcturus* (Greek for "bear watcher") is an orange giant with a magnitude of −0.06. Although cooler than the Sun, it is 20 times larger and more than 100 times brighter. At 36 light-years away, *Arcturus* is the closest giant star to Earth.

Virgo
The Virgin

To the Greeks, this zodiac constellation represents Persephone (per-SEF-o-nee), the daughter of Zeus and Demeter (dih-MEET-er), goddess of the Earth. Hades (HAY-deez), god of the underworld, fell in love with Persephone (represented in the heavens by **Virgo**) and stole her away to be his wife. Demeter was so upset that she could not perform her earthly duties. The weather chilled, and nothing would grow. To resolve matters, Zeus decided that Persephone should spend half of the year with her husband and half with her mother. When Persephone is in the underworld, her mother is sad, so the winds of autumn blow and the snows of winter cover the land. When Persephone returns to her mother, Earth enjoys spring and summer.

    Virgo is often shown with a sheaf of wheat in her hand. Within this spike of wheat grows *Spica* (SPY-kuh), the brightest star in this faint constellation. You can find it by using the Big Dipper to point the way. After you "arc" to *Arcturus*, follow the same curve to *Spica*, the next brightest star in line. *Spica* (Latin for "ear of wheat") is about 220 light-years away.

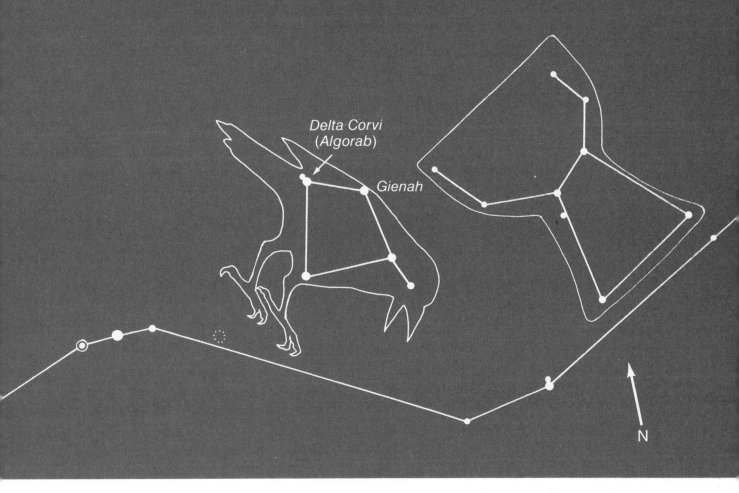

Corvus
The Crow

According to Greek myth, a crow was sent to get a cup of water for Apollo, the Sun god. The crow, Corvus, flew to a spring on Earth and was about to fill its cup when it spied a fig tree nearby. The hungry crow decided to wait until the fruit was ripe enough to eat before returning with the water. But soon Corvus realized that Apollo might be angry, so he came up with a plan. He pulled a water snake from the spring, carried it and the cup to Apollo, and blamed the serpent for the delay. But Apollo saw through the lie and threw everything into the sky, forming three constellations: **Hydra**, the serpent; **Crater**, the cup; and **Corvus**, the crow.

You can find the little constellation **Corvus** near **Virgo** by continuing the arc through *Spica* for about another 15 degrees. **Corvus** is also called Emansor, or "one who lingers too long." The brightest star in **Corvus** is *Gienah* (JIN-uh), a blue-white giant that, with a magnitude of 2.6, is 1,200 times brighter than our Sun. *Delta Corvi* (also known as *Algorab*) is a wide **binary star** (two stars that revolve around a common point) that can be easily seen with a telescope. The brighter of the two stars has a magnitude of 3.1. It is 100 times brighter than its companion.

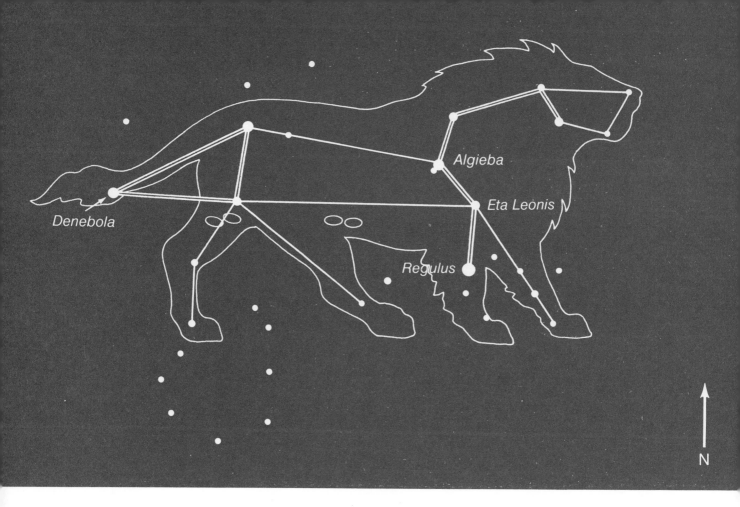

Denebola

Algieba

Eta Leonis

Regulus

N

Leo
The Lion

Both the Greeks and the Sumerians identified this constellation as a lion. The Greeks believed that Leo battled their hero, Heracles (HAIR-uh-kleez), while the Sumerians thought it was a fabled beast killed by their hero Gilgamesh (GIL-guh-mesh).

To find **Leo**, a constellation of the zodiac, use the two stars that make up the back of the Big Dipper's bowl as the pointers. Follow the line they form to about 40 degrees below the bottom of the dipper, directly on the line of the ecliptic. The stars at the head of this constellation form a bright, reversed question mark. At the bottom of the question mark is a brilliant blue-white star called *Regulus* (RAY-guh-lus), which marks the lion's heart. The Babylonians called *Regulus* "the king" and believed it ruled the heavens. Above *Regulus* is the hot, white supergiant *Eta Leonis* (AY-tuh lee-OH-nis), and at the lion's shoulder you will find *Algieba* (al-JEB-uh), a very beautiful binary star. *Denebola* (deh-NEB-oh-luh), Arabic for "the lion's tail," is a blue-white star with a magnitude of 2.1.

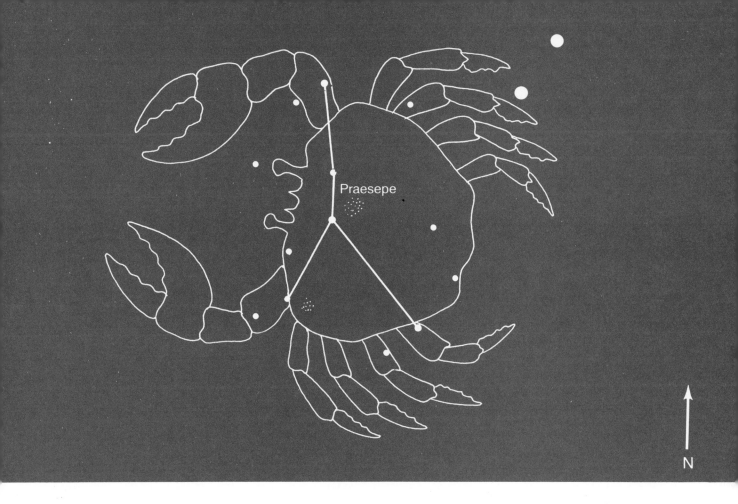

Praesepe

N

Cancer
The Crab

In Greek mythology, this crab was said to be one of the many beasts that battled the hero Heracles. During a ferocious struggle between Heracles and the nine-headed monster Hydra, the goddess Hera sent the crab to pinch the warrior so he would lose. But Heracles destroyed both the crab and Hydra and tossed them into the sky. Hera rewarded the crab's bravery by giving it a permanent place there.

Cancer (which means "crab" in Greek) is the faintest of the 12 traditional constellations of the zodiac. But on a clear, moonless night in a place away from city lights, it is not too difficult to locate because **Leo** gazes directly at it. There is a special treat within the body of the crab—Praesepe (pray-SEP-ee), the Beehive cluster. Praesepe is an **open cluster**, or group, of young stars that were all probably born at about the same time some 600 million years ago. The cluster is about 520 light-years away and although faint, it is visible to the naked eye. When Galileo focused his telescope on Praesepe, he counted more than 40 stars in this group. With modern binoculars or a small telescope, you can see at least 75 stars. And with a larger instrument, you can see about 350!

31

Summer Star Map
(June–September)

How to use this map:
Turn this star map so that the direction you face matches the direction of the constellations you can read. An easy way to do this is to identify known stars close to the horizon and then line up your map.

Scorpius

Sagittarius

Libra

Aquila

Hercules

Corona Borealis

Boötes

Lyra

WEST

Virgo

Draco

Cepheus

Leo

Ursa Minor and Little Dipper

Polaris

Ursa Major and Big Dipper

Scale of Star Magnitudes:
Seasonal Star Charts

- **0–1** First and most bright
- **2**   Second brightest
- **3**   Third brightest
- **4**   Fourth brightest
- **5**   Fifth and least bright

Milky Way

32

NORTH

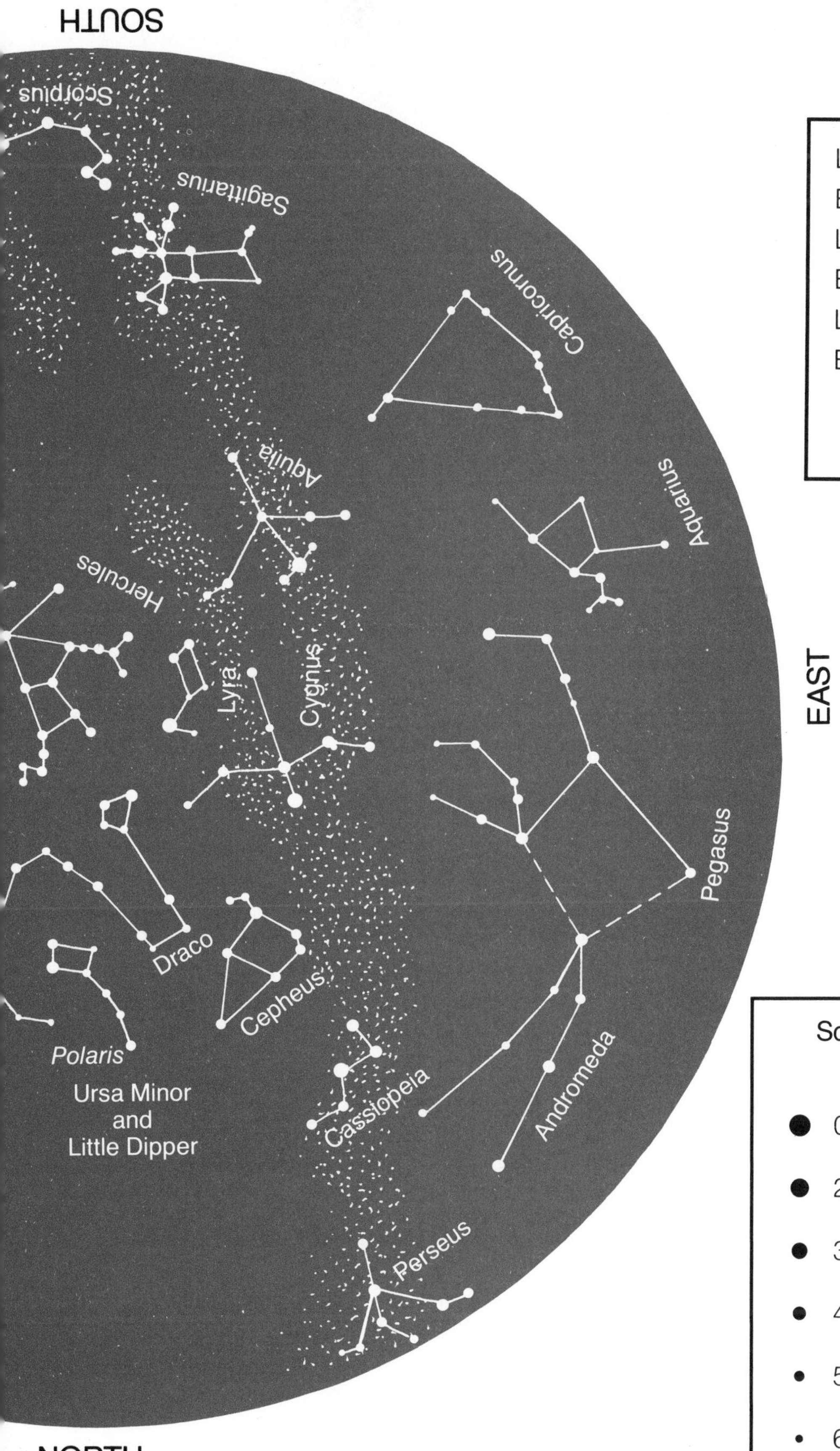

Scorpius

Sagittarius

Capricornus

Aquila

Aquarius

Hercules

Lyra

Cygnus

Pegasus

Draco

Cepheus

Andromeda

Polaris

Ursa Minor
and
Little Dipper

Cassiopeia

Perseus

EAST

Late June	12 p.m.
Early July	11 p.m.
Late July	10 p.m.
Early August	9 p.m.
Late August	8 p.m.
Early September	7 p.m.

Add one hour for
daylight-saving time

Scale of Star Magnitudes:
Individual Star Maps

- ● 0–1   First and most bright
- ● 2   Second brightest
- ● 3   Third brightest
- ● 4   Fourth brightest
- ● 5   Fifth brightest
- · 6+   Sixth and least bright

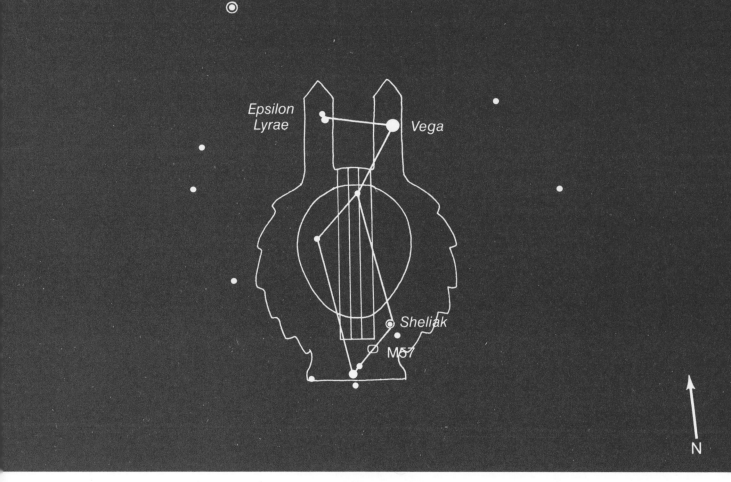

Lyra
The Lyre

Lyra (LY-ruh) represents the musical instrument of Orpheus (OR-fee-us), son of Apollo. When his wife, Eurydice (yuh-RID-uh-see), died, Orpheus went to the underworld to beg for her return. He played his lyre so sweetly that Hades agreed to return Eurydice, but on one condition: Orpheus could not look at her as they traveled to the outer world. But as the couple neared the surface, Orpheus turned to be sure Eurydice was there, and she slipped back to the land of the dead forever. Orpheus, heartbroken, also died. His lyre now glitters among the stars.

To find **Lyra**, look for the blue-white giant *Vega* (VEE-guh), which is almost directly overhead and the brightest star in the summer sky. *Sheliak* (SHEL-yak) is a set of three stars that orbit around each other (two of these stars are only 22 million miles apart). As the stars orbit each other, they appear as an **eclipsing variable star**. A **planetary nebula** is not easy to find, even with a telescope, but quite near *Sheliak*, with close attention you can spot M57 (also known as the Ring nebula). One of the best-known multiple-star systems is *Epsilon Lyrae* (EP-sih-lon LIH-ray), or the Double-Double. If you have very good eyesight you can see two of the components with the naked eye. With a telescope, you can make out all four.

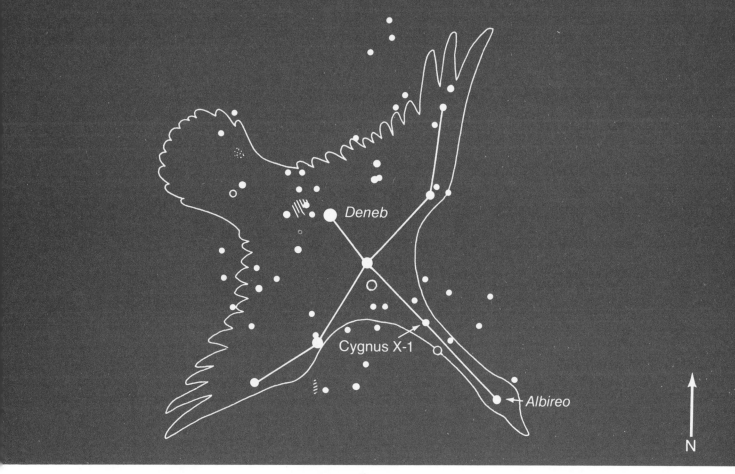

Deneb

Cygnus X-1

Albireo

N

Cygnus
The Swan

The Greek story of Cygnus (SIG-nus) is another sad tale. One day Phaethon (FAY-ih-tun), the young son of Helios (HEE-lee-us), the Sun god who was replaced in later myths by Apollo, asked his father if he could drive the chariot of the Sun across the sky. Helios reluctantly agreed. Soon after Phaethon began the journey, he lost control of the spirited horses. The chariot burned a wide glowing streak across the sky (the Milky Way). Then it passed too low over Africa and created the Sahara. To stop the destruction, Zeus had to kill the boy, and Phaethon's body tumbled into a river. Every day, Phaethon's best friend, Cygnus, sat on the riverbank and cried from grief. To ease his pain, the gods placed Cygnus in the sky, where he appears in the form of a swan.

    The constellation **Cygnus** is also called the Northern Cross. *Deneb* (DEN-eb), a blue-white giant with a magnitude of 1.3, is at the northern tip of the cross. Even though *Deneb* is about 2,300 light-years away, it is one of the 15 brightest stars in our sky. At the foot of the Northern Cross is the star *Albireo* (al-BEER-ee-o), a **visual double star** (a binary star that, to the naked eye, appears as one star). Within this constellation is also Cygnus X-1. Although we cannot see it, we know it is there because it is a powerful source of X-ray radiation. In fact, scientists think that at the heart of Cygnus X-1 there may be a black hole.

Altair

Eta Aquilae

M11

N

Aquila
The Eagle

The ancient Greeks, Arabs, and Turks all thought that the stars of **Aquila** (uh-KWIL-uh) formed an eagle. To the Chinese and Japanese, this constellation's brightest star, *Altair* (al-TAIR), was husband to Chih Nii (chee NYEE), the goddess of weaving. Chih Nii, represented by the star *Vega*, is separated from her husband by a great river in the sky—the Milky Way. Even today in Japan there is a special day dedicated to this husband and wife. For centuries it has been believed that messages thrown into any river would reach this lonely couple, because legend has it that all rivers of the world eventually empty into the Milky Way.

   Altair, at the head of the eagle, is 16 light-years away and 10 times brighter than our Sun. It is a rapidly rotating blue-white star with a magnitude of 0.8. *Eta Aquilae* (AY-tuh uh-KWIL-ay) is a cepheid variable star that can be seen with the naked eye. Watch it closely for about a week to notice that it shifts from bright to dim and back again. Follow the tail of **Aquila** and you will find M11, an open cluster that is a real treat to see through a telescope.

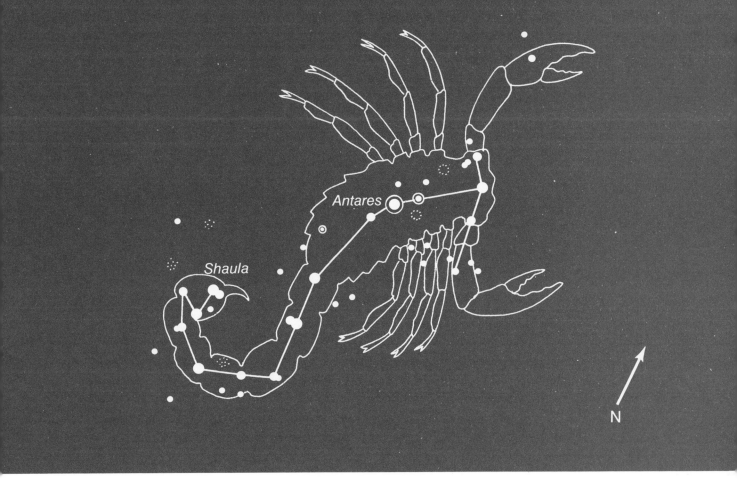

Scorpius
The Scorpion

Scorpius (SKOR-pee-us), a constellation of the zodiac, is one of the few constellations in which the star pattern looks very much like the thing for which it is named—in this case a gigantic scorpion. The Greeks told the tale of a hunter named Orion (or-EYE-un) who bragged that he could kill all the animals in the world if he wanted to. A goddess of the Earth became angry when she heard this, so she sent a scorpion to sting Orion to death. But the hunter escaped into the sea. When Orion finally died, the goddess Artemis placed him among the stars, where the scorpion still stalks him.

To find **Scorpius**, trace an arc from **Aquila**'s tail, through M11, then continue for about 40 degrees. Reddish *Antares* (an-TAR-eez), a magnitude-0.9 supergiant, represents the heart of **Scorpius**. This star, which is about 520 light-years from Earth, has a diameter about 400 times larger than that of our Sun! A **variable star**, *Antares* has a period of about five years. At the tip of the scorpion's tail are two stars. The brighter one is *Shaula* (SHOW-luh), which is Arabic for "the sting."

37

M23

M22

M20

M8

Kaus
Australis

N

Sagittarius
The Archer

Five stars in the zodiac constellation **Sagittarius** (saj-ih-TAIR-ee-us) form a bow and arrow aimed at the heart of **Scorpius**. The owner of the bow and arrow is the centaur Chiron (KAY-ron). (A centaur—a creature of Greek mythology—is half man/half horse.) However, many observers claim that this constellation is a steaming teapot! The "steam" is formed by the Milky Way galaxy, which is a wide, bright band in **Sagittarius**. This band is the best view we have of the billions of stars in the center of our galaxy (although much of the view is blocked by huge interstellar clouds of gas and dust).

At the bottom of the archer's bow is the 1.8-magnitude blue-white giant *Kaus Australis* (KOWS aws-TRAY-lus). If you look at the area above **Sagittarius** under clear, dark conditions, you may see the Lagoon nebula (M8), a glowing cloud of gas and dust that is barely visible to the naked eye. However, you will need a telescope to locate the Trifid nebula (M20). Two exciting star clusters, M22 and M23, also appear in this area. M22, the closest **globular cluster** to our solar system, can be seen with binoculars, while the open cluster M23 is visible with a telescope.

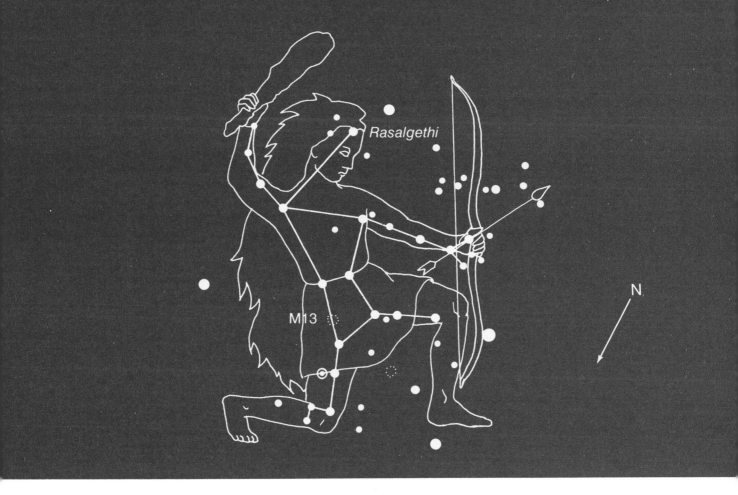

Hercules
The Kneeler

Follow the ecliptic away from **Sagittarius** and toward **Lyra** to find the dim constellation **Hercules** (HER-kyoo-leez), sometimes called the Phantom. In Greek and Roman mythology, Hercules (the Latin name for Heracles) was a hero of tremendous strength. He is often shown kneeling in the sky near the head of **Draco** (the Dragon) and facing **Aquila** (the Eagle) and **Cygnus** (the Swan).

One of the largest red supergiants visible to us with the unaided eye is *Rasalgethi* (raz-el-GEE-thee). Its name is Arabic for "the kneeler's head," and that is exactly where you will find it in this constellation. Although it is 600 times the diameter of our Sun, this variable star does not appear very bright because it is about 430 light-years from Earth. *Rasalgethi* is a binary star with a blue companion that can be viewed through a telescope. Along the line of the hero's body is a smudge of light that is dim but still visible to the naked eye. It is more than 25,000 light-years away, but with binoculars you can see what appear to be hundreds of stars bursting from a "fuzzy" center. This is M13, a globular star cluster.

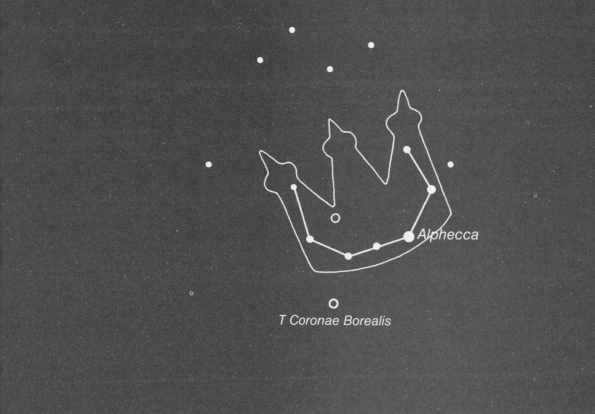

Alphecca

T Coronae Borealis

N

Corona Borealis
The Northern Crown

Corona Borealis (kor-OH-nuh bor-ee-AL-iss), nestled between **Boötes** and **Hercules**, looks like a splendid jeweled crown. The story of how it came to be placed among the stars is from a Greek legend. A very beautiful woman named Ariadne (ar-ee-AD-nee) won the heart of the handsome god Dionysus. He revealed to her that he was a god and asked for her hand in marriage. Ariadne didn't believe he was telling her the truth, so to prove his love, Dionysus produced for her the loveliest crown in all creation. Dionysus and Ariadne were married and when Ariadne died, the crown was placed in the sky in her honor.

The brightest star in this constellation, *Alphecca* (al-FEK-uh) is called the Jewel in the Crown. In Arabic, its name actually means "the broken ring." It is a blue-white star with a magnitude of 2.2. In 1866, a distant star, normally too faint to be seen without a telescope, glowed brilliantly (at a magnitude of 2.0) just below the lower curve of the crown for about a week, then faded from sight. This star, known as *T Coronae Borealis*, appeared again in 1946. Scientists believe that this star undergoes explosions on its surface that cause it to glitter at almost 5,000 times its normal brightness. This may happen again, so keep an eye on that spot!

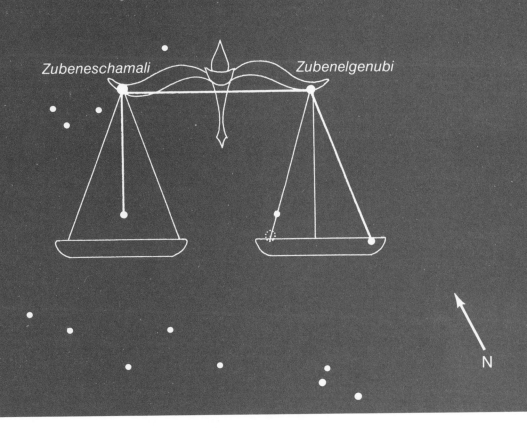

Libra
The Scales

Libra is the only constellation in the zodiac that does not represent a living thing. It is, instead, an instrument of balance. Although we know that the Earth revolves around the Sun, ancient peoples believed that the Sun moved around the Earth. The ecliptic, the Sun's apparent path through the sky, is tilted with respect to Earth's equator and to the imaginary equator above it in the sky (the **celestial equator**). For six months of the year, the Sun appears to be north of the celestial equator; for the other six months of the year, it appears to be south of the celestial equator. The days when the Sun seems to cross the celestial equator are the spring and fall **equinoxes** (EE-kwuh-nok-sez). At these times, the day and night are equal in length, or in balance. Several thousand years ago, the fall equinox occurred when the Sun was passing through **Libra**. Today the fall equinox takes place around September 21, when the Sun is in **Virgo**.

The two brightest stars in **Libra** are *Zubeneschamali* (zoo-ben-ESH-uh-MAL-ee) and *Zubenelgenubi* (zoo-ben-EL-jen-OO-bee). Whew! With binoculars you can see that the latter star is actually an extremely wide binary system. The brighter of the two visible stars is itself a binary but you won't be able to see its companion.

41

Fall Star Map
(September–December)

How to use this map:
Turn this star map so that the direction you face matches the direction of the constellations you can read. An easy way to do this is to identify known stars close to the horizon and then line up your map.

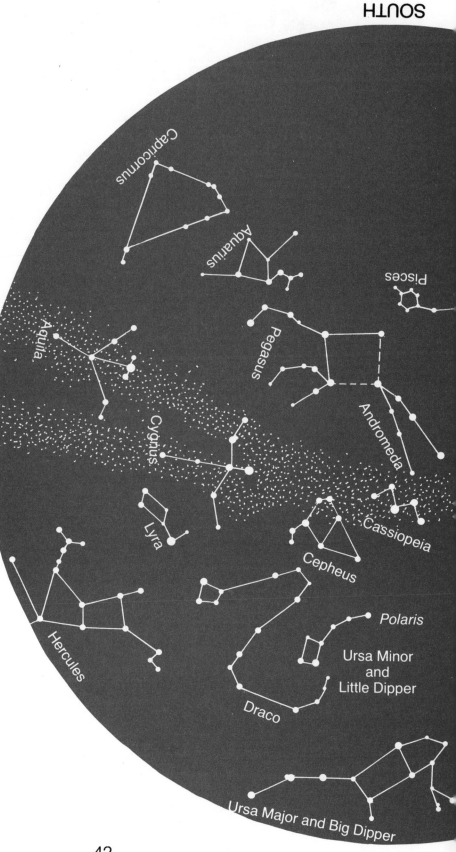

WEST

Capricornus

Aquarius

Pisces

Aquila

Pegasus

Andromeda

Cygnus

Cassiopeia

Lyra

Cepheus

Polaris

Hercules

Ursa Minor
and
Little Dipper

Draco

Ursa Major and Big Dipper

NORTH

Scale of Star Magnitudes:
Seasonal Star Charts

- ● 0–1   First and most bright
- ● 2   Second brightest
- ● 3   Third brightest
- ● 4   Fourth brightest
- · 5   Fifth and least bright

      Milky Way

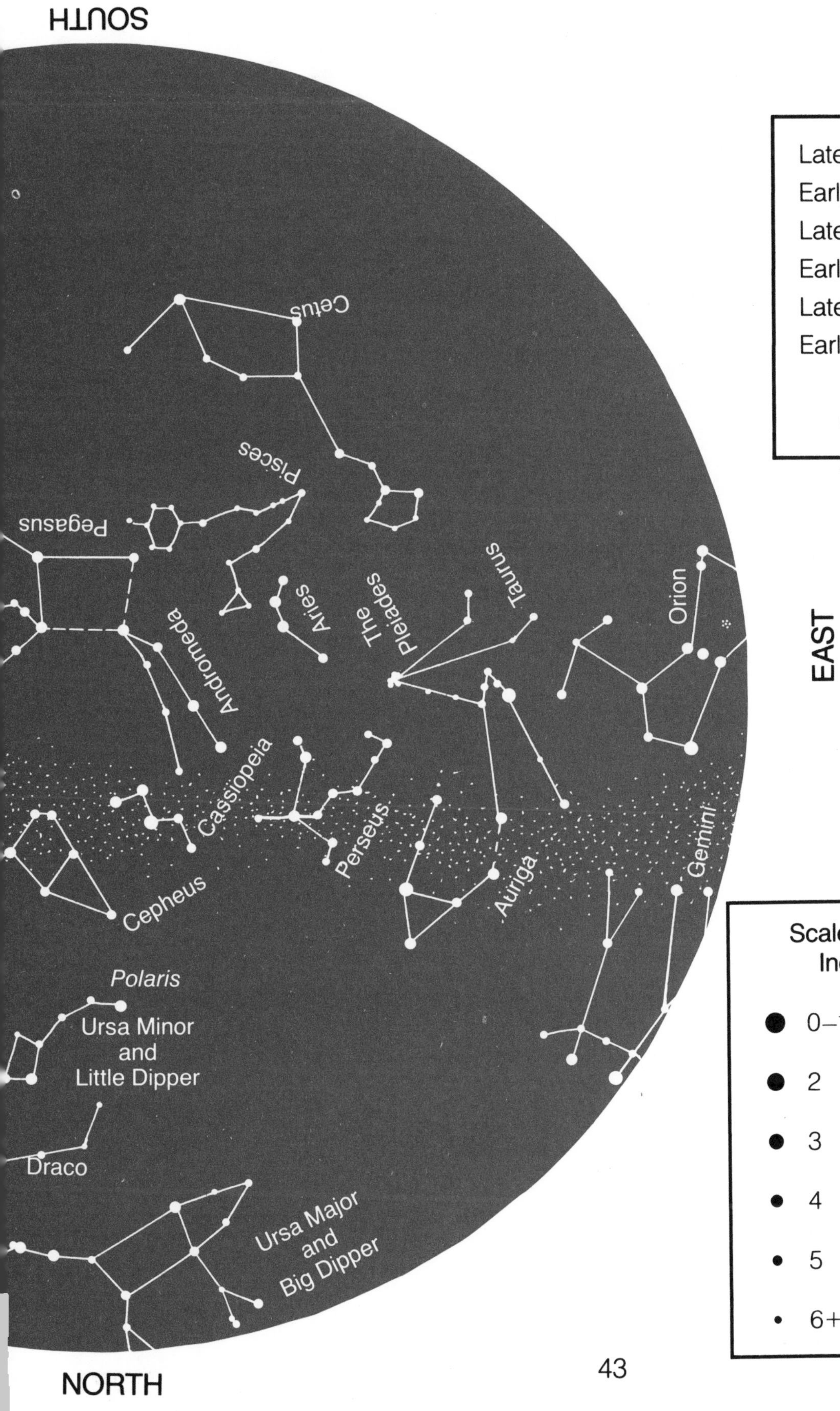

Cetus

Pisces

Pegasus

Andromeda

Aries

The Pleiades

Taurus

Orion

Cassiopeia

Perseus

Cepheus

Auriga

Gemini

Polaris

Ursa Minor
and
Little Dipper

Draco

Ursa Major
and
Big Dipper

EAST

Late September	12 p.m.
Early October	11 p.m.
Late October	10 p.m.
Early November	9 p.m.
Late November	8 p.m.
Early December	7 p.m.

Add one hour for
daylight-saving time

**Scale of Star Magnitudes:
Individual Star Maps**

● 0–1 First and most bright

● 2 Second brightest

● 3 Third brightest

● 4 Fourth brightest

● 5 Fifth brightest

• 6+ Sixth and least bright

Caph Shedar

Gamma Cassiopeiae

N

Cassiopeia
The Queen

Many of the fall constellations are connected by one Greek myth, the story of Perseus (PER-soos) and Andromeda (an-DROM-ud-uh). Andromeda's mother, Cassiopeia (kass-ee-oh-PAY-uh), was a fabled queen who often bragged about how beautiful she and her daughter were. (Indeed, she is often pictured sitting on a throne gazing at herself in a mirror.) Even though her bragging ended up causing a lot of trouble, the gods placed her in the heavens. For part of the year, **Cassiopeia** looks very royal on her throne in the sky, but the rest of the time she appears upside down as punishment for her boastfulness!

   During the fall, **Cassiopeia** forms an easy-to-recognize "W" in the sky. This constellation is also a reliable guidepost to other fall star groups. The brightest star in **Cassiopeia** is *Shedar* (SHEE-dar), which seems to have a pale pinkish tint. The next brightest star is *Caph* (KAF), Cassiopeia's "hand." *Caph* is a 2.3-magnitude blue-white giant. *Gamma Cassiopeiae* (kass-ee-oh-PY-ay), the middle star in the "W," is a blue giant variable star that unpredictably varies from magnitude 3.0 to 1.6.

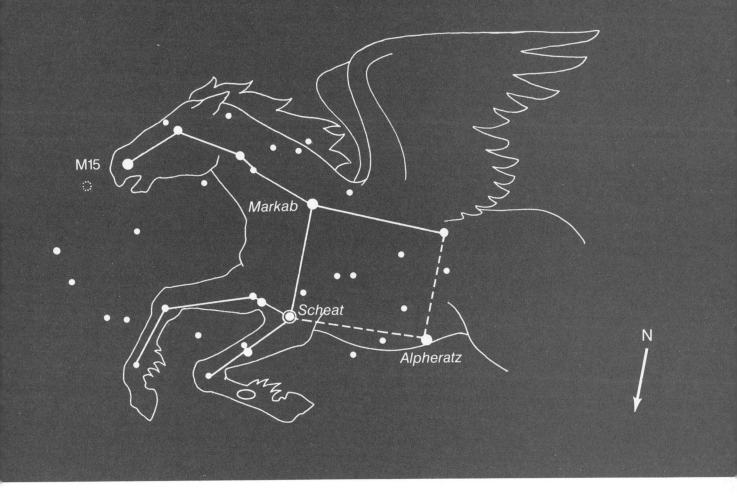

Pegasus
The Winged Horse

Pegasus (PEG-uh-sus) was a magnificent mythical winged horse. You can find the constellation of the same name by drawing a line from the center star in **Cassiopeia** through the lowest star, then down about 35 degrees. According to Greek legend, Pegasus was born from the blood of a monster—snake-haired Medusa (meh-DOO-suh). Medusa had once been a beautiful woman loved by the sea god, Poseidon (po-SY-don). When she was killed by Perseus, drops of her blood fell into the sea. In memory of his love for her, Poseidon mixed her blood with sea foam and from the mixture Pegasus was born.

    Pegasus runs across the sky with its head pointing down toward the equator. The four stars that mark its body make up the Great Square of **Pegasus**. One of these stars, *Alpheratz* (AL-fer-atz), is officially a part of the constellation **Andromeda**. Sometimes *Scheat* (SHEE-at) is the brightest star in **Pegasus**. But since it is an unpredictable variable star, *Scheat* becomes faint at times. Then *Markab* (MAR-kab), a 2.5-magnitude blue giant, becomes the brightest star in **Pegasus**. On a clear, dark night, using binoculars, you can also see a faint globular cluster of stars, M15, near the tip of the horse's nose.

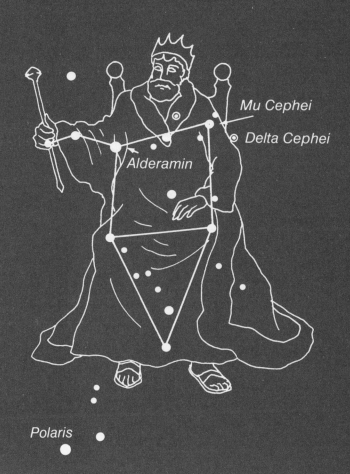

Mu Cephei

Delta Cephei

Alderamin

N

Polaris

Cepheus
The King

In Chinese myth, this constellation is called **Tsao Fu** (dow FOO), the charioteer. Tsao Fu bravely delivered his emperor to "the Western Paradise." As a reward, he was placed in the heavens. In Greek mythology, however, the constellation is named **Cepheus** (SEE-fee-us), after the husband of Cassiopeia. The king circles the sky at the side of his boastful wife.

This constellation looks more like a house with a pointed roof than a king. Just below the "house" is *Mu Cephei* (MYOO SEE-fee-eye), a red giant. *Mu Cephei* is the "eye" of **Cepheus**. This star, which is some 1,800 light-years away, is 14,000 times more powerful than our Sun! It is sometimes called the Garnet star because of its strong red glow. This constellation is also the location of a famous variable star first noted in 1784—*Delta Cephei* (DEL-tuh SEE-fee-eye). It changes magnitude from 3.6 to 4.3 over a very predictable period of 5 days, 8 hours, and 48 minutes. Since it was the first variable star of its kind to be discovered, stars similar to it are called cepheid variables. The brightest star in **Cepheus**, with a steady magnitude of 2.5, is *Alderamin* (al-der-AH-men). Its name is from an Arabic word that means "right arm," and it appears at the king's right shoulder.

46

Andromeda

Andromeda was the daughter of Cepheus and Cassiopeia. The queen's constant bragging angered Poseidon, god of the sea. He punished the family by sending the sea monster Cetus (SEE-tus) up and down the shore, raging and doing terrible damage. Poseidon agreed to stop the beast only if lovely Andromeda was sacrificed. There seemed to be no other alternative, so she was chained to a rock near the sea. In the sky, **Andromeda** still is chained and waiting to be rescued!

The arrow-shaped points of **Cassiopeia's** "W" aim toward **Andromeda**. The deeper of the two arrows points directly to the Andromeda galaxy (M31), which is the most distant object (2.2 million light-years away) that can be seen with the naked eye. This galaxy is much like ours, but slightly larger. With a telescope, you can distinguish the oval patch of light at its center. When you locate this remarkable sight, keep in mind that the light reaching us now from M31 left that far-off galaxy 2.2 million years ago! At that time, the earliest humans on Earth were probably first turning their gaze to the wonders of the night sky.

H Persei & Chi Persei

Mirfak

M34

Algol

N

Perseus

The hero Perseus, a son of Zeus, clashed with the horrible Medusa. Because her gaze could turn a human to stone, Perseus watched her reflection in his polished shield as they battled and so was able to defeat her. As he returned home, Perseus found the beautiful Andromeda chained to a rock by the sea. She tearfully told him her story, and Perseus promised to save her if he could have her hand in marriage. She agreed, he kept his promise, and the tale ends happily.

Perseus is usually shown holding the head of Medusa. Her eye is the red binary star *Algol* (AL-gol). As a companion star passes in front of *Algol* and blocks it from our view, the glowing "eye" seems to wink slowly! This wink lasts for about 10 hours. The brightest star in **Perseus** is the 1.8-magnitude blue-white supergiant *Mirfak* (MUR-fak), whose name is Arabic for "the elbow." Between **Perseus** and **Andromeda** is M34, an open cluster with individual stars that are visible through binoculars. A beautiful double star cluster (called *H Persei* and *Chi Persei*) can be found midway between *Mirfak* and the tip of **Cassiopeia**.

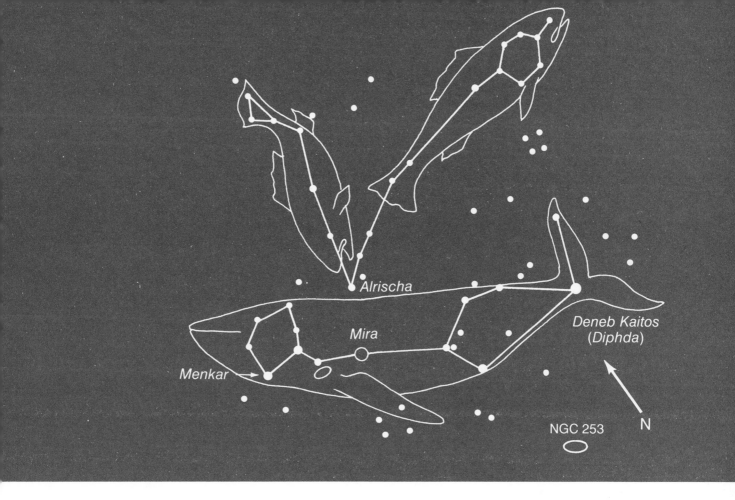

Cetus
The Whale

The sea monster **Cetus** is pictured as a whale because, until recent times, whales were considered to be sea monsters. **Cetus** swims along the celestial equator below **Andromeda**, its intended victim.

The brightest star in this large constellation is *Deneb Kaitos* (DEN-eb KAY-tos), which means "tail of the whale." This 2.0-magnitude yellow giant is also known as *Diphda* (DIF-duh). The next brightest star, *Menkar* (MEN-kar), is a 2.5-magnitude orange giant near the creature's nose. Its name means "the nose of the whale." Within **Cetus** is also a red variable star, *Mira* (MEER-uh), or "wonderful star." Don't be surprised if you can't find it, because *Mira* can be seen for only about 2 months during its 11-month cycle. *Mira's* magnitude ranges widely, from 9.5 to 3.0! Just above *Mira* twinkles a greenish-white star called *Alrischa* (al-REE-shuh). This star forms the knot that joins the two fish of the nearby zodiac constellation **Pisces** (PY-seez). **Cetus** is also near the galaxy NGC 253, which can be easily viewed with a telescope. Appearing just below *Deneb Kaitos*, this galaxy looks something like a miniature version of the Andromeda galaxy.

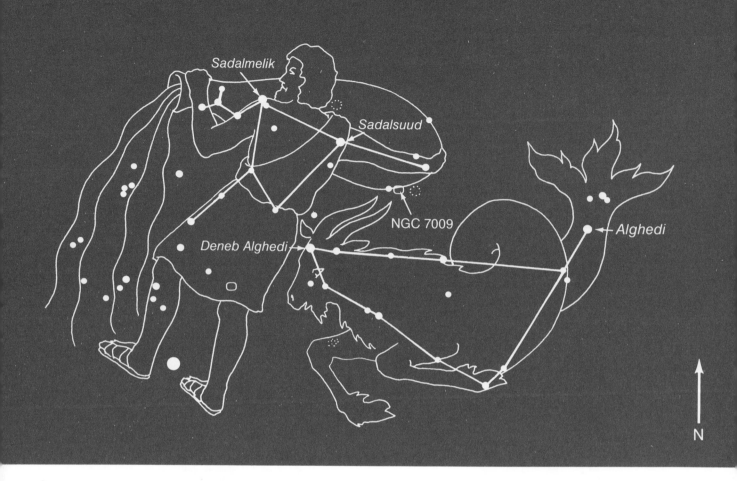

Sadalmelik
Sadalsuud
NGC 7009
Deneb Alghedi
Alghedi
N

Capricornus
The Goat

Aquarius
The Water Bearer

Dim members of the zodiac, **Capricornus** (cap-rih-KORN-us) and **Aquarius** (uh-KWAYR-ee-us) appear close together in the sky. Capricornus was the half goat/half fish form taken by a Greek god at the dawn of time, when the gods fought against giants. Frightened by the giant Typhon, the god Aegipan (EE-jih-pan) jumped into a river. The part of his body that remained above the surface became a goat, and the part below the surface turned into a fish.

    Capricornus and **Aquarius** are associated with water because a few thousand years ago the Sun passed through these constellations during the rainy season. When **Capricornus** and **Aquarius** rose in the sky, farmers knew to expect rain.

    Between these two constellations is NGC 7009, the Saturn nebula. Through a telescope it appears as a greenish oval. In **Capricornus**, look for *Alghedi* (al-JED-ee), an optical double star visible to the naked eye. Also visible, and brighter, is *Deneb Alghedi*, a 2.9-magnitude blue-white giant. The Arabs thought certain stars in **Aquarius** were lucky. Yellow *Sadalmelik* (sah-dal-MEL-ik) means "the lucky one of the king." *Sadalsuud* (sah-dal-SOOD) means "the luckiest of the lucky."

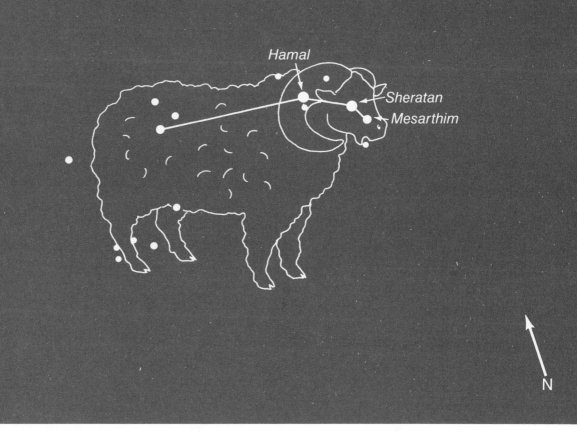

Aries
The Ram

Aries (AIR-eez) is traditionally listed as the first of the constellations of the zodiac. Two thousand years ago, the spring equinox occurred while the Sun was in **Aries**. The beginning of the spring season was signaled by the Sun's crossing of the celestial equator from the southern to the northern half of the sky. Because of the slow wobble of the Earth (precession), over thousands of years the time of the spring equinox has changed. It now occurs on March 21, when the Sun is in **Pisces**.

    Aries represents a magical ram whose golden fleece was sought by Jason and the Argonauts of Greek myth. The horns of the ram are marked by *Hamal* (huh-MAL), a 2.0-magnitude yellow giant, and *Sheratan* (sher-AY-tan), a slightly fainter blue-white star. The Greeks thought *Hamal* was a very important star. They even built several sacred temples in such a way that, at certain times of the year, the great star could be seen through the doors of these temples. If you view **Aries** through a small telescope, you will see that *Mesarthim* (meh-SAR-thim) is a visual double consisting of twin stars that may be a binary pair, but scientists aren't quite certain of that yet.

Winter Star Map
(December–March)

How to use this map:
Turn this star map so that the direction you face matches the direction of the constellations you can read. An easy way to do this is to identify known stars close to the horizon and then line up your map.

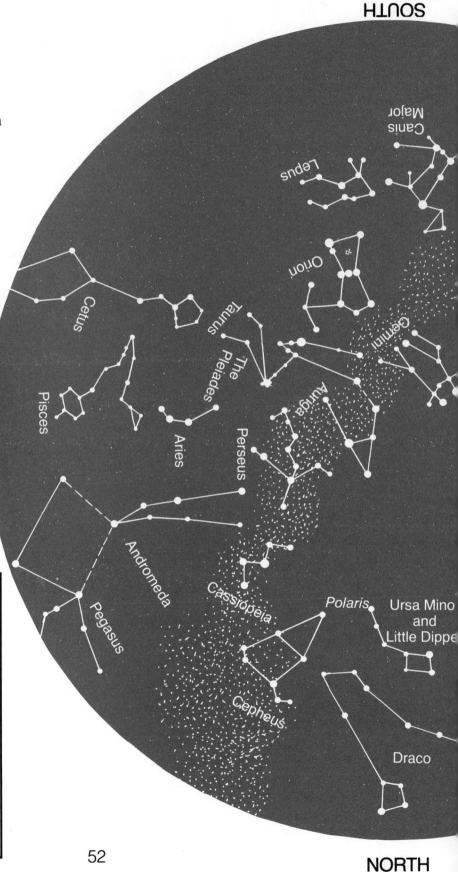

Scale of Star Magnitudes: Seasonal Star Charts		
●	0–1	First and most bright
●	2	Second brightest
●	3	Third brightest
●	4	Fourth brightest
·	5	Fifth and least bright
		Milky Way

Canis Major

Lepus

Orion

Canis Minor

Hydra

Taurus

Gemini

Cancer

Leo

Auriga

Polaris

Ursa Minor
and
Little Dipper

Ursa Major and
Big Dipper

Draco

EAST

Late December	12 p.m.
Early January	11 p.m.
Late January	10 p.m.
Early February	9 p.m.
Late February	8 p.m.
Early March	7 p.m.

Add one hour for
daylight-saving time

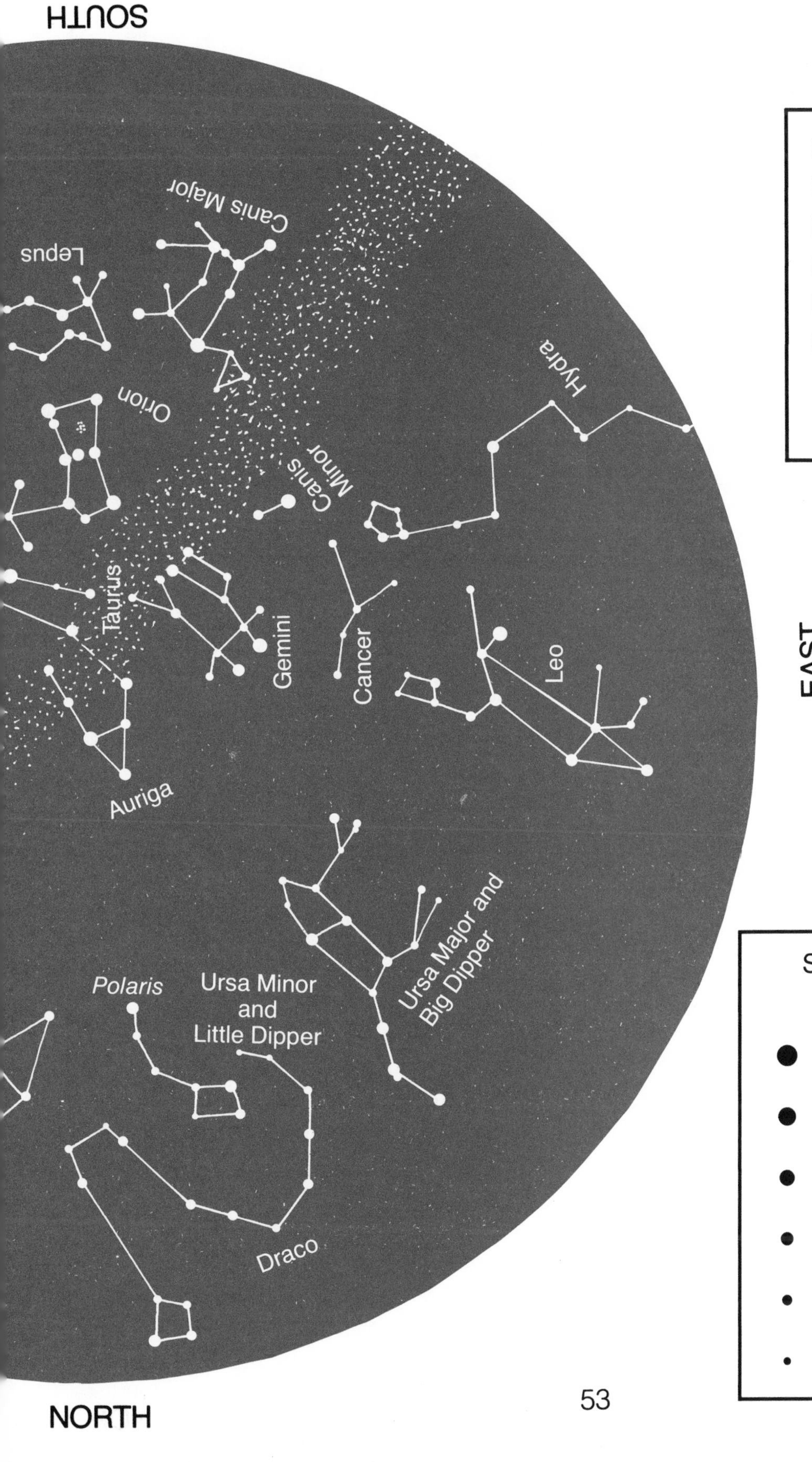

Scale of Star Magnitudes: Individual Star Maps

● 0–1 First and most bright

● 2 Second brightest

● 3 Third brightest

● 4 Fourth brightest

• 5 Fifth brightest

• 6+ Sixth and least bright

NORTH

53

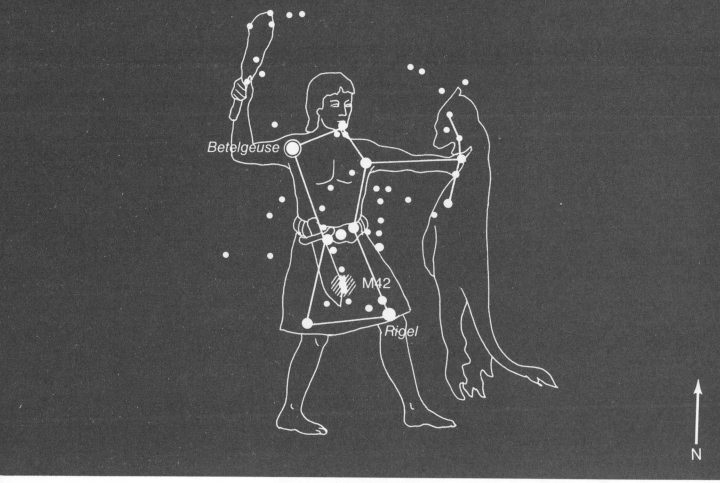

Orion
The Hunter

The winter skies are easily read thanks to pointers such as the Big Dipper, **Cassiopeia**, and **Orion** (or-EYE-on). Of these, the hunter is the only one that is not visible all year long. It appears in the sky for about five months, and then disappears below the horizon.

Orion contains two of the sky's 15 brightest stars. Deep-red *Betelgeuse* (BEE-tul-joos) is the shoulder of the giant. It is a variable star that swells and shrinks over a cycle of about six months. *Rigel* (RY-jel), which means "the foot," is 900 light-years away, but it still glows brightly. This is because *Rigel* is nearly 60,000 times more luminous than our Sun, 80 times larger, and more than 25 times more massive!

Orion's belt is formed by three stars. Hanging from the belt is a sword, and halfway down the blade is a fuzzy greenish blur. This is the Orion nebula (M42), an immense cloud of gas and dust that is a full 25 light-years across. Many stars are being formed in this swirling cloud. The ultraviolet light of these hot stars causes their gas clouds to glow like a flourescent advertising sign. With a telescope, you should be able to see the *Trapezium* (truh-PEE-zee-um), four stars glittering in the nebula.

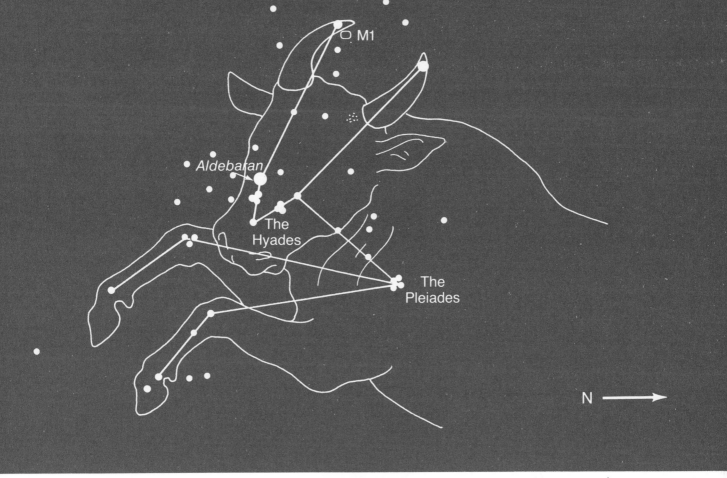

Taurus
The Bull

About four thousand years ago, the spring season began when the Sun was in the constellation of the bull. Every spring the Nile River overflowed its banks, depositing rich soil and silt on Egyptian farmland and helping the crops to flourish. That may be why the bull, the symbol of the zodiac constellation we now call **Taurus**, was sacred to the Egyptians.

Draw a line through **Orion**'s belt to the west about 20 degrees, and you will find *Aldebaran* (al-DEB-uh-ran). This 0.9-magnitude red giant is the bull's right eye. Use binoculars to examine more closely a cluster of stars called the Hyades (HY-uh-deez), which makes up the "V" shape of the bull's face. Only 140 light-years distant, this distinct cluster of stars is very close to our solar system. Near the bull's right horn is the Crab nebula (M1), the remnants of a supernova witnessed by Chinese astronomers in 1054. The nebula is now nearly 10 light-years across and is still spreading at a rate of about 50 million miles a day!

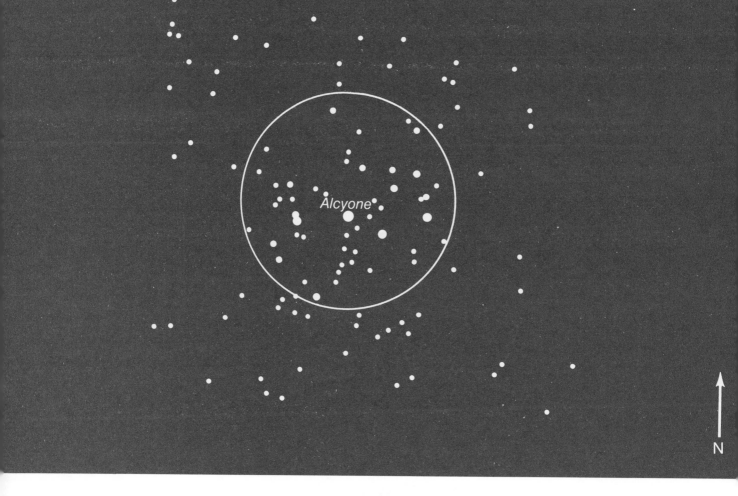

The Pleiades

The Pleiades (PLEE-uh-deez) is not a constellation but a twinkling group of stars forming the left shoulder of **Taurus**. A Polynesian myth holds that the Pleiades was once a single large beautiful star. This star often bragged about its looks. The god Tane (TAH-nay) grew tired of listening, so he threw the giant star *Aldebaran* at the boastful Pleiades, which burst into smaller pieces. It is said that the little stars later chattered among themselves about how much more beautiful they were now that there were so many of them!

   Although up to nine stars in this group may be seen with the naked eye, the Pleiades is often called the Seven Sisters (perhaps because when the group was first named, some were a little fainter than they are today). Believe it or not, there are actually *five hundred* or more stars in this cluster that is about 410 light-years from Earth. The brightest star in the Pleiades is *Alcyone* (al-SY-o-nee), which is 10 times the diameter of our Sun and a thousand times brighter. Interestingly, you can see the Pleiades better if you look at the cluster from the corner of your eye rather than directly.

56

Canis Major
The Great Dog

Canis Major (KAY-nis MAY-jor) and **Canis Minor** are **Orion**'s faithful hunting dogs. The brightest star in our sky is −1.5-magnitude *Sirius* (SEER-ee-us), also called the Dog star, in **Canis Major**. The diameter of blue-white *Sirius* is about twice that of our Sun. This star first peeks above the eastern horizon on late summer mornings just before sunrise, and long, hot summer days are often called "dog days." *Sirius*, which is only nine light-years from Earth, appears fairly low above the horizon. You can find it in **Canis Major** by following the downward tilt of **Orion**'s belt toward the horizon for about 20 degrees. Three stars form the dog's hindquarters: the supergiants *Aludra* (uh-LOO-druh), *Wesen* (WEZ-en), and the blue-white giant *Adhara* (uh-DAR-uh). *Adhara* is the second brightest star in this constellation.

Sirius is a binary star. Its companion, *Sirius B*, is a massive white dwarf star nicknamed the Pup. It is so dense that a teaspoonful of this "star stuff" would weigh about a ton. You won't be able to see the Pup, even with a telescope. Also in **Canis Major** is *Mirzam* (MUR-zam). When *Mirzam* appears above the horizon, *Sirius* is not far behind.

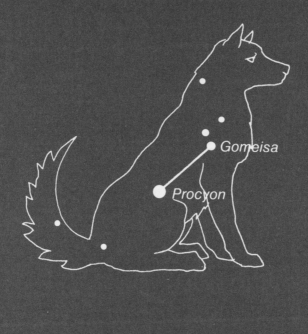

Gomeisa

Procyon

N

Canis Minor
The Little Dog

The band of light that is the Milky Way separates the star *Procyon* (PRO-see-on) in **Canis Minor** (KAY-nis MY-nor) from *Sirius* (in **Canis Major**). A sad Arab legend explains why this is so. The two stars were young sisters who decided to follow their older brother into the fields one day and became lost. When they neared a wide river in the sky—the Milky Way—the older sister, Sirius, jumped into the water and swam to the other side. Procyon, afraid of the water, stayed behind and so was forever parted from her sister. Procyon's tears are said to add to the waters that cause the yearly flooding of the Nile.

To find **Canis Minor** draw a line from **Orion**'s fainter shoulder star to *Betelgeuse*, then straight outward for about 30 degrees. The brightest star in this little group is yellowish-white *Procyon*. This 0.4-magnitude star is only 11 light-years away. Like *Sirius*, *Procyon* is a binary star, with a smaller white dwarf companion that is too faint to see even with a small telescope. *Gomeisa* (go-MY-zuh), the only other bright star in this constellation, is about 10 times farther away than *Procyon*.

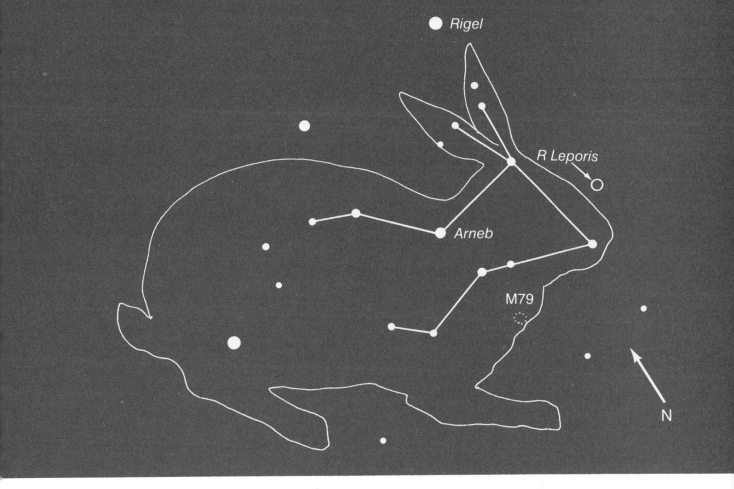

Lepus
The Hare

Hunting dogs seem to like chasing rabbits and hares. The two devoted dogs of **Orion**, the hunter, are no different. Scampering just out of reach of the dogs **Canis Minor** and **Canis Major** is **Lepus** (LEE-pus), the hare. It is a very small constellation, but it is not too difficult to find. Appearing just beneath the feet of **Orion**, it is about 10 degrees directly below *Rigel*. Its brightest star, *Arneb* (AR-neb, Arabic for "the hare"), is a blue-white supergiant with a magnitude of 2.1. Now some 950 light-years distant, this star is racing away from Earth at about 15 miles per second.

Through a telescope, the hare **Lepus** seems to be leaping over a tiny, hazy patch in the sky. This is M79, a large, distant globular cluster of stars. Perhaps the most interesting star in this group is a faint variable star near the hare's nose called *R Leporis* (lee-POR-us). It is also called *Hind's Crimson Star*, after the English astronomer who discovered it. If you are lucky enough to spot it with your telescope, you will be looking at one of the reddest visible stars in the sky.

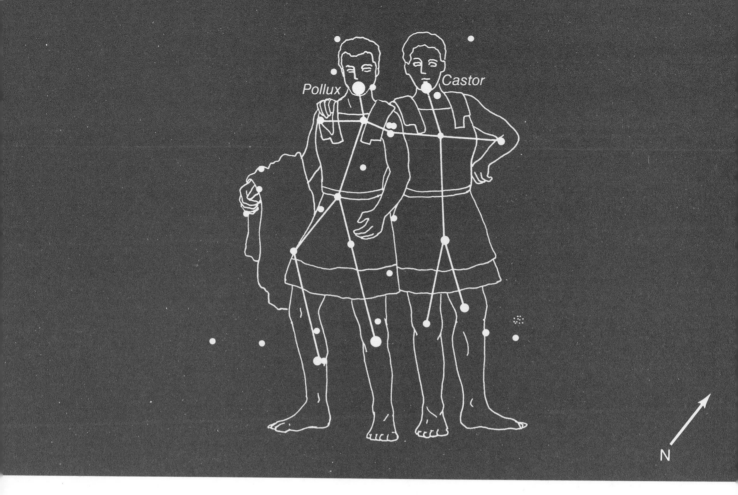

Gemini
The Twins

This constellation of the zodiac is represented by an odd pair of twins, Castor and Pollux. Although (according to Greek myth) these twins were born at the same time, they had different fathers! Pollux (PAHL-uks) was the son of Zeus and a mortal woman named Leda. Castor was the son of Leda and her true husband, King Tyndareus (tin-DEHR-ee-us). Pollux was immortal but Castor was not. When Castor died, Pollux begged Zeus to let them stay together. The only thing Zeus could do was place them side by side in the sky.

   Castor and *Pollux* are the brightest stars in **Gemini** (JEM-ih-nee). Orange-tinted, 1.0-magnitude *Pollux* is slightly brighter and closer to us, but 1.6-magnitude *Castor* leads as the constellation rises. To find the twins, draw a line from the uppermost star in **Orion**'s belt through *Betelgeuse* and toward the ecliptic for about 40 degrees. Through a telescope, *Castor* appears as a double star. However, an instrument called a spectroscope, which examines light energy from a star, shows us that *Castor* is actually a system of three binary pairs of stars!

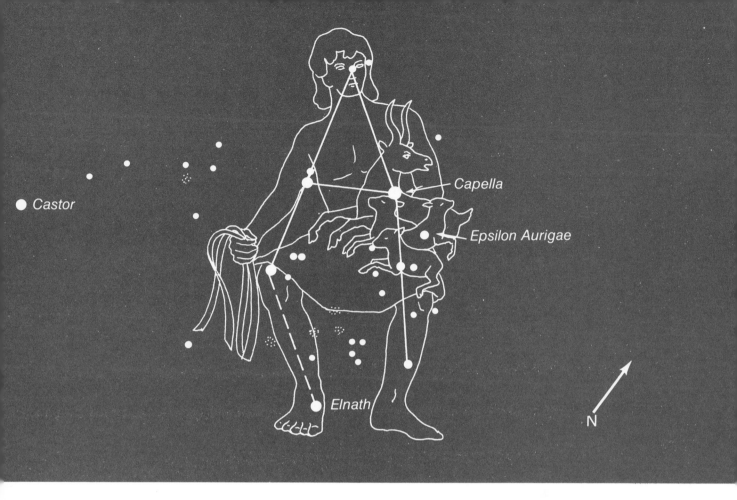

Castor

Capella

Epsilon Aurigae

Elnath

N

Auriga
The Charioteer

A charioteer is a person who drives an open, horse-drawn vehicle. The constellation **Auriga** (or-EYE-guh) shares the star *Elnath* (el-NATH) with **Taurus**. The star forms the western foot of the charioteer and the northern horn of the bull. **Auriga** is usually shown as a man with reins ready, but without horses or chariot. In his right arm, the charioteer is carrying a goat and her kids.

Capella (kuh-PEL-uh), whose name is Latin for "little she-goat," is the brightest star in **Auriga**, with a magnitude of 0.1. This star is near the charioteer's shoulder and is part of a close binary pair. South of *Capella* are three tiny stars that represent her kids. The top of this triangle is *Epsilon Aurigae* (EP-sih-lon AWR-ih-gay), a supergiant eclipsing binary star that is 200 times larger and 60,000 times more luminous than our Sun, and more than 2,000 light-years away from us. This star's companion is a mystery "object" that passes in front of the star every 27 years. This object is huge (almost a billion miles across), but comparatively cool. It may be a dim, aged red supergiant, or some form of disk-shaped space cloud, but no one is certain.

Glossary

absolute magnitude   A measure of the true brightness of a star calculated as if the star were a certain distance (10 parsecs) from Earth.

aphelion   The point farthest from the Sun in a planet's or comet's orbit.

apparent magnitude   The measure of how bright a star looks to an observer on Earth.

astronomical catalogues   Catalogues of celestial objects, such as galaxies, nebulae, and star clusters. The objects are identified by letters. The three main catalogues used are Messier's Catalogue (M), the New General Catalogue (NGC), and the Index Catalogue (IC).

axis   An imaginary line through the center of an object. The object seems to turn on its axis. Earth, for example, spins on its axis once every 24 hours.

binary star   See **double star**.

black hole   A small, incredibly dense object in space. This unusual object is so dense that nothing, not even light, can escape its gravitational pull.

celestial equator   An imaginary line in the heavens above Earth's equator. It divides the celestial sphere into northern and southern hemispheres.

celestial sphere   An imaginary sphere, like a shell, around the Earth. To an observer, objects in the night sky appear to be fixed on this sphere.

cepheid variable star   See **variable star**.

density   The ratio of mass to volume. If two objects are the same size but one is denser, the denser object will have more mass.

diameter   The distance of a straight line through the center of a circle or sphere from one side to the other.

double star   A pair of stars. There are many kinds of double stars. A **binary star** is a pair of stars that revolve around a common center of gravity. A **visual double star** is a binary star that can only be resolved through a telescope but, to the naked eye, appears as one star. An **eclipsing binary star** is a pair of stars in which one star passes between its companion star and an observer, causing the companion to appear to vary in brightness. An **optical double star** is a pair of stars that, to the naked eye, appear to be very close together but actually are not. They are merely in the same line of sight.

eclipsing binary star   See **double star**.

eclipsing variable star   See **variable star**.

ecliptic   The apparent yearly path of the Sun as it seems to move across the celestial sphere.

equator   An imaginary line around a body such as the Earth, dividing it into two equal halves.

equinox   One of the two times during the year, in spring and in fall, when day and night are equal in length.

globular cluster   A large, spherical cluster of older stars.

gravity   The force of attraction between an object and every other object.

hemisphere   One-half of a sphere or globe.

horizon   The point at which the sky and Earth seem to meet.

interstellar space   The space between stars in a galaxy.

lens   A curved piece of glass or plastic that bends light rays traveling through it.

light-year   A measure of the distance that light travels through a vacuum in one year. One light-year is about 6 trillion (6,000 billion) miles.

mass   The amount of matter in an object.

matter   Any substance that has mass and takes up space. Everything in the universe is made of matter.

myth   A story using imaginary places or characters to explain something.

nebula   A cloud of dust and gas in space. Under certain conditions, new stars are born within some nebulae. A **planetary nebula** is a cloudlike "shell" of gas ejected from a giant star before it collapses inward.

open cluster   A large, irregular-shaped cluster of young stars.

optical double star   See **double star**.

orbit   The path of an object that is moving around another object in space.

parsec   A unit of measurement in astronomy. One parsec equals 3.26 light-years.

perihelion   The point closest to the Sun in a planet's or comet's orbit.

planetary nebula   See **nebula**.

supernova   A huge explosion that is usually caused by the collapse of a giant star under the weight of its own gravity.

variable star   A star that varies in brightness. There are several kinds of variable stars. A **cepheid variable** is a star that dims and brightens very regularly over short periods of time. It can be used by astronomers to determine the distances to star clusters or galaxies that contain them. An **eclipsing variable** is a star whose brightness only appears to change because it is temporarily dimmed by a passing companion star.

visual double star   See **double star**.

zenith   To an observer, the point in the sky that is directly overhead.

Index